ACTIVATING
RESTORATION
PROMISES

ACTIVATING RESTORATION PROMISES

Seven Promises of the Lord

I have seen his ways, and will heal him; I will also lead him, and restore comforts to him and to his mourners. (Isaiah 57:18)

James A. Durham

XULON PRESS ELITE

Xulon Press Elite
2301 Lucien Way #415
Maitland, FL 32751
407.339.4217
www.xulonpress.com

Unless otherwise indicated, Bible quotations are taken from THE HOLY BIBLE, NEW KING JAMES VERSION. Original work copyright © 1979, 1980, 1982 by Thomas Nelson, Inc. Quotations designated (NIV) are from THE HOLY BIBLE: NEW INTERNATIONAL VERSION®. NIV®. Copyright © 1973, 1978, 1984 by International Bible Society. Quotations designated (KJV) are from the KING JAMES VERSION Quotations designated (CJB) are from the COMPLETE JEWISH BIBLE. Copyright 1998 by David H. Stern, Published by Messianic Jewish Publishers, 6120 Day Long Land, Clarksville, MD 21029, (410) 531d-6644 Quotations designated (ONMB) are taken from THE ONE NEW MAN BIBLE, copyright © 2011 William J. Morford. Used by permission of True Potential Publishing, Inc. Quotations designated (ESV) are from The Holy Bible, English Standard Version. Copyright © 2001 by Crossway Bibles, a division of Good News Publishers.

Printed in the United States of America.

Paperback ISBN-13: 978-1-6322-1493-5
eBook ISBN-13: 978-1-6322-1494-2

Table of Contents

Introdcution: Seven Promises of Restoration xi

1. Activating Your Restoration 1

2. "I Will Sprinkle Clean Water On You" 24

3. "I Will Cleanse You" 46

4. I Will Give You a New Heart 70

5. I Will Put My Spirit Inside You 90

6. I Will Save You From Uncleanliness 111

7. I Will Summon the Grain 131

8. I Will Multiply Your Fruit 149

9. I Have Spoken and I Will Do It 175

10. They Will Know That I Am The Lord 192

11. For My Holy Name's Sake 214

12. Double Portion Restoration 241

13. More Restoration Promises 260

14. Restoration Gathering 277

Summary 293

Acknowledgements

The entire contents of this book came as a special gift of revelatory understanding from the Lord. Therefore, I want to express my thanks first and foremost to Him for providing the wisdom and knowledge for this book and for the inspiration and encouragement He provided along the way to complete the project. The Lord is good and His love and mercy endure forever. Without Him, none of our works would succeed. It is with gratitude and praise that I acknowledge all He has done to make this book possible.

I also want to acknowledge the invaluable assistance I received from my extremely blessed, highly favored and, powerfully anointed wife, Gloria. Without her encouragement and assistance, this book could never have been completed. I am also grateful for her dedicated and tireless assistance in proofreading the book and confirming the accuracy of the scriptural references. In addition to my wife, I want to acknowledge my daughter, Michelle, who remains a constant and consistent cheerleader throughout the process of all my writings. Anytime I needed encouragement, I had only to turn to either of these two wonderful ladies. I am so thankful to the Lord that He placed them in my life and constantly blesses me through their love and support!

Endorsements

"Do you feel there is something more available for you to fulfill your destiny? There is! This is the season of your full restoration. And James Durham's revelation will allow you to finish well!

Sid Roth,
Host, *It's Supernatural!*"

"God is in the business of restoration, and James Durham has captured the heart of God for His promises to be released into this generation.

James Durham will give you the keys and walk you through the activation process to receive that which was lost in the Natural and Spiritual realm.

Ken Peltier,
Director of Partner Relations
Sid Roth's *It's Supernatural!*"

Seven Promises of Restoration

When I began to write this book the question came to me again as it did with the first book in this series: "Why should you invest your time and energy reading this book?" I kept asking myself this question, and then I took it to the Lord. After meditating and praying for an answer to this question, I received three reasons for you to spend time studying the revelation in this book.

1. The Lord wants you to have personal knowledge, wisdom, and revelation of the promises He has given.

2. The Lord wants to increase your effectiveness in the great harvest by training and equipping you in this process.

3. The Lord wants you to activate His powerful gifts for restoration in your own life and ministry. In other words, He wants to bless you beyond measure.

The first book in this series focused on the seven promises of the Lord for the redemption of His people. Some questions came to me as I was finishing that book. What comes after redemption? What is the Lord's plan for us after we receive and activate the fullness of His redemptive promises? I prayed and asked the Holy Spirit to help me understand. The answer came very quickly. The Lord brings restoration to His people to bless them. The restoration of His people also comes for His name's sake. In other words, the Lord is glorified and He is well pleased when He redeems and restores His people.

Once again, I went back to the message I received from the Lord. As I meditated on these powerful promises of the Lord, I began to hear the Lord speaking to me. A progressive revelation began to be released to me which continued for several weeks. At the beginning of this process, I heard the Lord saying to me, "Many people pray as if they're begging me to do what I have already said I will do. Instead of praying like this, they need to believe my words. They need to receive and activate what I have already promised." I immediately understood that there was little or no faith in the prayers begging the Lord to do what He has already promised to do. The Lord is inviting us to activate these promises again in our generation, and as we see them manifest, to increase our faith in His Word and His promises. At the heart of this revelation is a call, which is being released by the Lord for His people, to have faith in His Word. It is time for us to put our trust in His promises.

Why should you study these promises of the Lord? We are well into the season of the great harvest which Yeshua described in John 4:35, "*Do you not say, 'There are still four months and then comes the harvest'? Behold, I say to you, lift up your eyes and look at the fields, for they are already white for harvest!*" We need to open our eyes right now to things happening in the spiritual realm. The great harvest isn't something coming in the distant future. It is here right now. If it had already arrived when Yeshua was giving this teaching, the season is far spent now. Amen?

In this season the Lord is calling us back to a deeper understanding of the basic beliefs and doctrines of our faith. Like a good sports team, we must constantly go back to the fundamentals of the process. As you improve and strengthen these fundamental principles of the harvest, the Lord prepares you both physically and spiritually to be more effective in your Kingdom ministry. Many believers act as if they are completely unaware of these messages from the Lord. Now is the time to get back to the foundational principles, ideas, and beliefs of our calling. I remember a call to return to the basics given by the writer of the book of Hebrews.

> *Therefore, leaving the discussion of the elementary principles of Christ, let us go on to perfection, not laying again the foundation of repentance from dead works and of faith toward God, of the doctrine of baptisms, of laying on of hands, of the resurrection of the dead, and of eternal judgment. And this we will do if God permits.* (Hebrews 6:1-3)

SUMMARY OF THE SEVEN PROMISES OF RESTORATION

Ezekiel 36:25-30 (CJB)

Promise 1: *"Then I will sprinkle clean water on you, and you will be clean;"*

Promise 2: *I will cleanse you from all your uncleanness and from all your idols."*

Promise 3: *"I will give you a new heart and put a new spirit within you; I will take the stony heart out of your flesh and give you a heart of flesh."*

Promise 4: *"I will put My Spirit inside you and cause you to live by My laws, respect my rulings and obey them. You will live in the land I gave to your ancestors. You will be my people, and I will be your God."*

Promise 5: *"I will save you from all your uncleanliness."*

Promise 6: *"I will summon the grain and increase it, and not send famine against you."*

Promise 7: *"I will multiply the yield of fruit from the trees and increase production in the fields, so that you never again suffer the reproach of famine among the nations.*

Throughout the Bible, the Father continues to release powerful "I will" promises to His people. Over and over the Lord released these amazing and wonderful promises of restoration to succeeding generations. In Ezekiel chapter 37, the Lord gave His prophet an illustration of how powerful His promises can be. He carried the prophet in the spirit to a valley filled with extremely dry bones and asked him if these bones could live again. In the natural it is impossible, but for God all things are possible. Then Ezekiel obediently prophesied to the bones and they came back to life as a mighty army for the Lord. This vision was given to challenge Israel to look beyond their circumstances and realize that the Lord could and would bring them back from despair and hopelessness and renew their spiritual strength to empower them to rise again and reach their amazing kingdom destiny.

Just before the Lord released this powerful and well-known message of His plan to miraculously bring back the vitality and strength of the nation of Israel, He commanded Ezekiel to prophesy over the mountains of Israel. Ezekiel trusted the Lord and spoke the prophetic words which Father God had given him. Think about this. At that time, Ezekiel was in captivity hundreds of miles from Israel. How could his words spoken in captivity have any effect on the mountains of Israel? In the natural, this plan doesn't make sense, but Ezekiel was not willing to let these doubts hold him back. In faith, he released these powerful God-given decrees to the distant mountains of Israel. The Lord used Ezekiel's act of faith to open and begin to release a great season of blessing and restoration for His people.

When you look at your circumstances, you may think they are too big or too terrible for anything to change them. This is a lie from the enemy. With the Lord, all things are possible. Your circumstances cannot be greater than a valley filled with very dry bones. Trust the Lord. He can overcome every barrier which challenges you in the natural and release a mighty wave of spiritual power to release and restore you, your family, and your ministry. Trust the Lord even when His word to you seems strange and impossible. When the Lord asks you to speak to the distant mountains of your circumstances, trust Him. Speak His word and His decrees. Then stand in faith until the restoration of the Lord manifests. Amen?

The promises of restoration are sevenfold as with the promises of redemption given in the book of Exodus. Consider this: In the same way the promises of redemption given through Moses are for you, these fresh promises of restoration given through Ezekiel are also for you. Build up your faith to receive them and activate them in your own life and ministry. Dare to believe and allow yourself to receive all that the Lord wants to release to you.

THIRTEEN BONUS PROMISES OF RESTORATION

The Lord's heart for redeeming His people becomes clear as you study the messages He has given for us through both the major and minor prophets. (Major and minor refer to the size of their writing not the quality of their work. For example,

Hebrew scholars believe that Hosea was the greatest of all the prophets, but little of his work is in our Bible because much of his 90 plus years of service as a prophet consisted of speaking only to people who lived in those generations.) Over and over the Lord has released promises for the restoration of His people in every generation. From this, we see that the Lord is very committed to releasing full restoration for you in the natural as well as in the spiritual realm. The promises have been given and need only to be believed, received, and activated. We don't have to beg for what He has already promised to give. The power of His word is already present in these promises. When you speak them aloud and claim them, that great power in the Word of God is released once again for you, your family, and your ministry.

In the book of Isaiah, the Lord released another set of 7 powerful promises for the restoration of His people. This time they are His promises for another generation in a future time of restoration. Read the promises given through Isaiah in the two passages below. Then add to these the third passage giving six more restoration promises. Then speak all of them aloud to activate God's power. Next, claim them for yourself and those you care for. Finally, begin to give Him praise and glory while you wait for them to manifest.

> *Fear not, for I am with you; be not dismayed, for I am your God. **I will** strengthen you, yes, **I will** help you, **I will** uphold you with My righteous right hand.* (Isaiah 41:10)

*For **I**, the Lord your God, **will hold** your right hand, saying to you, 'Fear not, **I will** help you.' "Fear not, you worm Jacob, you men of Israel! **I will** help you," says the Lord and your Redeemer, the Holy One of Israel. "Behold, **I will** make you into a new threshing sledge with sharp teeth; you shall thresh the mountains and beat them small, and make the hills like chaff.* (Isaiah 41:13-15)

*The poor and needy seek water, but there is none, their tongues fail for thirst. **I, the Lord, will** hear them; **I,** the God of Israel, **will not** forsake them. **I will** open rivers in desolate heights, and fountains in the midst of the valleys; **I will** make the wilderness a pool of water, and the dry land springs of water. **I will** plant in the wilderness the cedar and the acacia tree, the myrtle and the oil tree; **I will** set in the desert the cypress tree and the pine and the box tree together, that they may see and know, and consider and understand together, that the hand of the Lord has done this, and the Holy One of Israel has created it.* (Isaiah 41:17-20)

A promise which has not been activated has little effect because the power of the Lord has not been released in it. Every promise of the Lord is filled with the potential to accomplish what He has spoken. "*So shall my word be that goeth forth out of my mouth: it shall not return unto me void, but it shall accomplish that which I please, and it shall prosper in the thing whereto I sent it.*" (Isaiah 55:11, KJV). Speak it aloud to release that potential in your life in this generation. Remember that you have the spiritual authority which has been given to you by the Lord: "*And the spirits of the prophets are subject to the prophets.*" (1 Corinthians 14:32) Speak to your spirit now to release the power of God to activate His promises in your heart, soul, and body. Amen?

In these last days, we need to be fully empowered by the Lord to be successful in His field of harvest. In other words, we need to be fully trained and equipped for the service of the Lord in this season (see Ephesians 4:11-17). In the following chapters, we will explore together the depth of the meaning and potential in His promises. The primary focus of this book is to assist you in seeing, receiving, and activating the Lord's promises of restoration. Consider what Yeshua said in Matthew 17:11-12, "*Jesus answered and said to them, "Indeed, Elijah is coming first and* **will restore all things**. *But I say to you that Elijah has come already, and they did not know him but did to him whatever they wished. Likewise the Son of Man is also about to suffer at their hands.*" Did you understand the extent of the Lord's promises for restoration given in that quote from Yeshua? He plans to restore all things. The work was completed through the ministries of both John the baptizer and Yeshua ha Messiach. The only thing remaining is for us to accept it by faith.

As the Children of Israel prepared to go into the land which the Lord had promised to them, Joshua gave the people a powerful reminder to help them build their trust in the Lord. Joshua reminded the people that the Lord had kept all His promises. To begin with, He had fulfilled all of the four primary promises for their redemption released to them in Egypt and during the exodus. Joshua said, *"Now I am about to go the way of all the earth. You know with all your heart and soul that not one of all the good promises the Lord your God gave you has failed. Every promise has been fulfilled; not one has failed."* (Joshua 23:14) Notice the double statement of Joshua. First, he says it in a positive way twice, and then gives it in another way: Not one of the Lord's promises failed!

These promises are given over and over in each succeeding generation. Now, they are being released to you and me. The Lord also gives us faith builders so we can put our trust in Him. He keeps His promises. First, we are given the testimony of Joshua immediately after the promises were fulfilled in his generation. We also have testimonies from many succeeding generations. As we move into the New Testament era, we are given another faith builder. Yeshua fulfills the Lord's promises of redemption and restoration. All God's promises are "Yes" in Yeshua.

> *For all the promises of God in Him* (Yeshua) *are Yes, and in Him Amen, to the glory of God through us.*
> (2 Corinthians 1:20)

REVIEW

LOOK AGAIN AT THE SEVEN PROMISES OF RESTORATION FOUND EZEKIEL 36:25-30 (CJB)

As I discussed above, one of the most well-known passages of scripture in the Bible is found in Ezekiel 37:1-10. Take a moment to think through this once again as a means of anchoring it in your mind and spirit. In this passage, you read the story about how the Lord told Ezekiel to speak to some dry bones scattered about in a large valley. This is often read or taught as a standalone story, however, the story began in the previous chapter as the Lord revealed His plan for the restoration of Israel.

In other words, in the previous message, the Lord had pre-pared the prophet for this mission of bringing dry bones back to life. In Ezekiel chapter 36, the Lord commands Ezekiel to prophesy over the mountains of Israel. At that time, Ezekiel was in captivity hundreds of miles from Israel. There was no way for him to travel back to Israel to complete this mission. He must speak from where he is and believe the Lord will act. This is faith. In this part of the scriptures, the Lord is revealing two very important spiritual facts to the prophet, Ezekiel. I wanted you to go through this again to get the two facts clearly in your mind.

First, time and distance do not affect the power of God released through His Word as well as through His prophets. Ezekiel didn't have to physically be in Israel to release a powerful move of the Spirit there. The second important fact is given to assist you in understanding the power of obedience. When Ezekiel obeyed the Lord and spoke the words he was given, his powerful God-given decrees opened a season of blessing and restoration for the entire nation. Think about what the Lord can do through you when you faithfully release His prophetic decrees.

This move of God didn't begin in the valley of dry bones. In the same way, it doesn't begin for you in your circumstances. Take your eyes off of your trials and troubles and grasp the Lord's promises given in His Word. Restoration begins with the Lord. His seven promises of restoration released in Ezekiel chapter 36 are for you to overcome your circumstances using the power of His promises. The thing for you to clearly understand here is that the promises of restoration are first released for people in the spiritual realm. After they are released in the spiritual realm, they begin to manifest in the natural.

These promises are sevenfold just like the promises of redemption given in the book of Exodus. This is important to understand. In book one of this series, ("Redemption,") I shared that all the promises of redemption given through Moses are also released by the Lord for you. In the same way, these promises of restoration are for you. You don't have to beg the Lord to give them to you. He has already given them to all His children in all generations. Your task now is to receive them and activated them by faith in your own life and ministry.

We all like the idea of restoration! Right? Consider this: the first five promises of restoration are for our cleansing. The Lord's first action is to cleanse us in spirit, soul, and body. Think about it! The Lord takes care of our spiritual needs before He releases these promises to manifest in the natural realm. Most people are not ready to operate fully in the spiritual realm because they are aware of their uncleanliness. When we are cleansed, we are spiritually ready to receive and activate all these powerful promises. Consider this point and compare it to the message found in Psalm twenty-four.

> *Who may ascend into the hill of the Lord? Or who may stand in His holy place? He who has clean hands and a pure heart, who has not lifted up his soul to an idol, nor sworn deceitfully. He shall receive blessing from the Lord, and righteousness from the God of his salvation. This is Jacob, the generation of those who seek Him, who seek Your face. Selah (Psalm 24:3-6)*

CHAPTER ONE

Activating Your Restoration

HOW CAN YOU ACTIVATE THIS IN YOUR PRAYERS?

I n the first book in this series "*Redemption*", I outlined the way David activated the promises of the Lord in His personal life as well as in his kingdom. He always began by praising God for who He is and what He does. He acknowledged the Lord as the keeper of promises. He concluded these psalms by worshipping the Lord for letting all these promises manifest in his life. As you study the writings of David, you gain an appreciation for why the Lord called him a man after His own heart.

And when He had removed him (King Saul), He raised up for them David as king, to whom also He gave testimony and said, 'I have found David the son of Jesse, a man after My own heart, who will do all My will.' (Acts 13:22)

I encourage you to study David's prayers to gain wisdom as you seek to be a man or woman after God's own heart. The majority of the "I will" statements in the Bible are made by the Lord. David learned from his study of the Torah the importance of these promises. As he became more and more like the heart of God, David began to make "I will" promises of His own. As you reflect on this remember the promise of Yeshua in John 14:12, *"Most assuredly, I say to you, he who believes in Me, the works that I do he will do also; and greater works than these he will do, because I go to My Father."* If you believe in Yeshua, you are gifted to do the works that He did. It is both your destiny and your purpose in the Kingdom of God on the earth. It is your time to make some "I will" promises just as David did. Begin now by saying David's promises aloud.

David's Six "I will" promises:

I will extol You, my God, O King; and I will bless Your name forever and ever. Every day I will bless You, and I will praise Your name forever and ever. Great is the Lord, and greatly to be praised; and His greatness is unsearchable. One generation shall praise Your works to another, and shall declare Your mighty acts. I will meditate on the glorious splendor of Your majesty, and on your wondrous works. Men shall speak of the might of Your awesome acts, and

I will declare Your greatness. They shall utter the memory of Your great goodness, and shall sing of Your righteousness. (Psalm 145:1-7)

Like David, we are also invited to make some heartfelt promises to the Lord. As you begin this practice, always remember that it is important to keep all promises and vows you make to the Lord. The thing to remember is that you should only make those vows which you are certain you can keep. Remember Solomon's warning in Proverbs 20:25, "*It is a snare for a man to devote rashly something as holy, and afterward to reconsider his vows.*" After making these six "I will" promises to the Lord, David continued to give Him even more praise. Once again, I recommend that you make these words of praise your own and activate them by speaking them aloud to the Lord right now. I recommend that you do this often by making this a part of your regular worship.

The Lord is gracious and full of compassion, slow to anger and great in mercy. The Lord is good to all, and His tender mercies are over all His works. All Your works shall praise You, O Lord, and Your saints shall bless You. They shall speak of the glory of Your kingdom, and talk of Your power, to make known to the sons of men His mighty acts, and the glorious majesty of His kingdom. Your kingdom is an everlasting kingdom, and Your dominion endures throughout all generations. (Psalm 145:8-13)

APPEAL TO HIS ATTRIBUTES
THROUGH PRAISE

Over time David, the man after God's own heart seems to flow more and more gloriously in his praises for the Lord. I believe that David had a lifestyle of praise which became his natural response toward everything the Lord said and did in his life. Praise became his second nature and he was truly gifted at it. I recommend you follow the same process of speaking the Lord's praise as a way to release the power in His promises. Read the next section of Psalm 45 aloud over and over until it becomes yours and opens the door for a lifestyle change of your own.

> *The Lord upholds all who fall, and raises up all who are bowed down. The eyes of all look expectantly to You, and You give them their food in due season. You open Your hand and satisfy the desire of every living thing. The Lord is righteous in all His ways, gracious in all His works. The Lord is near to all who call upon Him, to all who call upon Him in truth. He will fulfill the desire of those who fear Him; He also will hear their cry and save them. The Lord preserves all who love Him, but all the wicked He will destroy. My mouth shall speak the praise of the Lord, and all flesh shall bless His holy name forever and ever.* (Psalm 145:14-21)

Are you hearing the Lord speaking promises to you? If not, perhaps this is a good time to begin using these activation methods in your times of worship. Ask yourself this question: How do I normally respond in praise to Him for all the good things promised and delivered to me? Remember James 1:17, "*Every good gift and every perfect gift is from above, and comes down from the Father of lights, with whom there is no variation or shadow of turning.*" There is no variation in the Lord. He promises and He delivers on what He has spoken to you.

When there appears to be a variation, the problem is not with the Lord. It is with us. The real problem is our failure to believe, receive, and activate the promises. This failure results in our limiting what we receive from the Lord. Believe this now: "*Blessed be the God and Father of our Lord Jesus Christ, who has blessed us with every spiritual blessing in the heavenly places in Christ.*" (Ephesians 1:3) How many spiritual blessings has He promised? Some may answer; "some of them." Others may say "most of them." But the correct answer is "all" of them. He promised and He delivers all of His good things to us through Yeshua ha Messiach. Are you ready to activate more of His promises?

HOW DO YOU ACTIVATE HIS PROMISES?

As I shared in the introduction of the first book in this series, this is a question that emerged from the people with whom I first shared this message which I received from the Lord. I had an idea about this but had not fully worked it out in my mind. After a pastor in South Korea asked me this question, I began a biblical search for a clear answer from the Lord. As

I prayed, I asked the Holy Spirit to give me wisdom and revelation to fully understand how we can activate all the promise of the Lord given in His Word.

After praying, I started to think about some of the great prayers in the Bible. I asked myself and then I asked the Holy Spirit if any of these Biblical prayers focused on and activated specific promises of the Lord. As I continued this search, I discovered that many of the prayers in the Word of God are in the form of claiming what the Lord has promised. I was particularly drawn to the many recorded prayers of David. His prayers and the prayers of his son, Solomon, are great examples of this approach for activating the Lord's promises. For this study, I want to draw your attention once more to one particular prayer of David.

> *And now, O Lord God, You are God, and Your words are true, and You have promised this goodness to Your servant. Now therefore, let it please You to bless the house of Your servant, that it may continue before You forever; for You, O Lord God, have spoken it, and with Your blessing let the house of Your servant be blessed forever.* (2 Samuel 7:28-29)

David's approach demonstrates the use of a pattern of prayer which activates the Lord's "*I will*" promises. Notice that David first praises God for who He is. Then He praises Him for what He has done in the past. Finally, David refers to one of the Lord's "*I will*" promises and places a claim on it for both himself and His family. David concludes his prayer by giving the Lord praise. He adds some permanence to the process by calling the Lord's promise a blessing that will last forever. No wonder the Lord refers to David as a man after His own heart.

There is one more thing I want you to notice about David's way of praying. This is something common to most of his prayers. David begins to give the Lord praise and glory for fulfilling His promises even before they manifest in the natural. This is a powerful statement of faith. David was so confident in the Lord's fulfillment of His promises that He was able to give thanks before he saw any results. How about you? Can you receive the promises by faith and continue to give Him thanks and praise until they manifest? Can you do this without wavering?

These are the spiritual steps of David which you can implement in your own prayer life. I will explain this in more detail in the section below. For now, consider how important it is to respond to the Lord's promises in faith. Don't wait to believe until after you see it manifest. Let it manifest because you stand in faith by giving the Lord thanks and praise for the blessings before you see any results. How long should you do this? My answer is – as long as it takes. Never stop! Never give up! Never quit! Amen?

CONSIDER YOUR PRAYERS

I suggest that you begin to intentionally apply this method to your prayers. One way to do this is to ask yourself some key questions. Begin by asking yourself, "How many of my prayers are like David's prayers?" Next ask: "How many of my prayers place a claim on what the Lord has promised?" Finally ask, "How many blessings have I missed because I didn't receive and activate His promises?" I encourage you to ask other questions as you are led by the Holy Spirit to help you understand what the Lord is saying to you. Be as honest with yourself as possible. Remember, you are the only one who will hear the answers to these questions. It is okay if the Lord hears you because He already knows. I believe this is the only effective way to open your spirit and your mind to change.

One of the best ways to learn a new prayer method is to practice it over and over. As you do this, it becomes your natural way of approaching the Lord. It is my practice to base everything on the Word of God. I believe that the Lord had these promises written in the Bible because He meant for you and me to receive and activate them in our generation. By faith, I believe that every promise in the Word of God is for me. I also believe all these promises are for you. I hope and pray you will receive all of them and begin activating them now.

To activate these promises you must intentionally receive them by faith. I do this by saying them aloud over and over as I place a claim on them for my life and ministry. I keep saying them until they take root in my heart. I encourage you to do the same. This is very different from begging the Lord to act on your behalf. You are not begging, but claiming the promises He has already released for your own life and ministry. You can begin now by claiming the promises in the next two passages of scripture. Remember to read them aloud and speak out your willingness to receive them in the mighty name of Yeshua ha Messiach. Then give Him thanks and praise even before they manifest.

> *Most assuredly, I say to you, he who believes in Me, the works that I do he will do also; and greater works than these he will do, because I go to My Father. And whatever you ask in My name, that **I will do**, that the Father may be glorified in the Son. If you ask anything in My name, **I will do it**.* (John 14:12-14)

> *Behold, **I give you the authority** to trample on serpents and scorpions, and over all the power of the enemy, and nothing shall by any means hurt you.* (Luke 10:19)

As you claim these promises, you are activating them in your own life. This is the kind of prayer the Lord was telling me to implement in my life and to share with others. Here is something to consider: if these prayers are answered, think about how this might change your life and ministry. Pause for a moment and reflect on this. If you begin to operate in this authority and with these promises, how will your life and ministry be transformed? Think about the power and authority which will be released as you do His Kingdom business. Remember Jesus' instruction to his followers (this includes you) in the passage below. You are to receive "*power.*" Amen?

And being assembled together with them, He com-
manded them not to depart from Jerusalem, but to
wait for the Promise of the Father, "which," He said,
"you have heard from Me. For John truly baptized
with water, but you shall be baptized with the Holy
Spirit not many days from now." Therefore, when
they had come together, they asked Him, saying,
"Lord, will You at this time restore the kingdom to
Israel?" And He said to them, "It is not for you to
know times or seasons which the Father has put in
His own authority. But you shall receive power when
the Holy Spirit has come upon you; and you shall be
witnesses to Me in Jerusalem, and in all Judea and
Samaria, and to the end of the earth." (Acts 1:4-8)

The same amazing spiritual excitement which I received from reading the seven promises in Exodus 6:6-8 happened to me as I studied the seven "I will" promises for Restoration in the book of Ezekiel. Over and over, I was drawn by the Holy Spirit back to the promises in the passage from Ezekiel Chapter Thirty Six. I began to understand more and more clearly that this in-depth study was becoming a series of books to train and equip the saints for a great end-time harvest. I also came to believe that the Lord wants others to experience what happens to me each time I read these promises. I believe the Lord wants you to have a similar experience of excitement as you read, receive, and activate His seven powerful promises of restoration for yourself.

I believe the Lord is challenging us to operate at a much higher level of faith. I believe He is encouraging us to put all His promises into action and not just casually read about them in the Bible. I believe the Lord is inviting us to experience a different type of prayer. He wants to activate the kind of prayer which releases His power through His Word. How about you? After reading this far, are you convinced and ready to receive the power and authority He is releasing to you? Are you ready to activate and operate at a higher level of anointing?

Once again, I am convinced that these words of promise need to be spoken aloud to activate the power which the Lord has placed in them for our benefit. I am reminded of a powerful teaching about this process of activation released through Paul in Romans 10:16-17, "*But they have not all obeyed the gospel. For Isaiah says, 'Lord, who has believed our report?' So then **faith comes by hearing**, and **hearing by the word of God**.*" It is a spiritual fact that faith comes by hearing. The voice you trust most is your own. As you speak these things aloud, allow your spirit to receive the Word of God, and trust what He is saying in all His promises. Allow His Word to activate His promises for you.

The first and essential step in effectively operating in this way is to know the promises. I make it a practice to note in my Bible each promise and to read over and over every "*I Will*" statement of the Lord. Another key is to understand clearly who is making the promises. This is why it is so important to spend much time in the Word of God. The Lord has provided both of these elements for us in His written word. One of the greatest self-revelations of the Lord is found in the book of Exodus.

> *Now the Lord descended in the cloud and stood with him there, and proclaimed the name of the Lord. And the Lord passed before him and proclaimed, "The Lord, the Lord God, merciful and gracious, longsuffering, and abounding in goodness and truth, keeping mercy for thousands, forgiving iniquity and transgression and sin, by no means clearing the guilty, visiting the iniquity of the fathers upon the children and the children's children to the third and the fourth generation."* (Exodus 34:5-7)

Hebrew scholars refer to this passage as the thirteen attributes of the Lord. He first revealed these attributes to us through Moses on Mount Sinai. On the mountain, Moses received the greatest revelation of the Father given to humanity up to that point. In this proclamation, the Lord tells us who He is and what He does. I encourage you to study this passage over and over as David did before he wrote his powerful prayers which are now available to us in the Psalms. As you read David's prayers, notice that he refers to portions of this revelation of the Lord's attributes time and again. He acknowledges who the Lord is and what He has done in the past. Then David places a claim on all these promises for the present and the future.

Are you claiming these promises for yourself, your family, and your ministry? Use David's example as a guide for your prayers. Claim the Lord's powerful promises of mercy, grace, and goodness. Claim the promises of patience and truth given to us by the Lord. Claim the forgiveness of iniquity, transgressions, and sin. As you practice this kind of prayer, you are planting in your own heart a powerful understanding of who the Lord is and what He does. You are building a powerful and effective level of faith which will open the doors of blessing and favor in your own life and work.

Think about this. In the New Testament, you can see Yeshua (Jesus' name in Hebrew) modeling these attributes of the Lord released to Moses on Mount Sinai. In Egypt, the Lord made a powerful decree. He declared to His people: "I AM the Lord!" Perhaps you are wondering about this as I did. I kept asking the Holy Spirit: Didn't they already know that He was the Lord? The answer I received from the Holy Spirit was that they had little or perhaps no understanding of what His decrees truly meant. At that time, they did not have a clear understanding of Who He was or want He did for them. It took centuries for people to understand the power in this decree. In the Old Testament (Genesis through Malachi), He repeats this decree at least one hundred and sixty-two times. It was soon after He made this powerful decree that they came to know the Lord as Adonai/Elohim. This awesome God of both mercy and justice was the one who then revealed His seven primary and powerful action promises for their redemption.

Think about this as you meditate on His promises. In the worst of times, the Lord released these promises to His people. They were in a really bad situation. They were slaves in Egypt and they were being greatly mistreated. Now a stranger had come to them declaring their release. It all sounded good, but after He met with Pharaoh things had only gotten much worse. Have you had an experience like this? You pray and believe you have been granted deliverance only to find that your situation seems to get worse. Have faith. The Lord sometimes operates this way so He can reveal His person and power to you and others around you. Don't give up! Don't quit! The Lord keeps His promises. The Lord's promises are activated when we become and stay obedient to Him:

> *Thus says the Lord of hosts: "If you will walk in My ways, And if you will keep My command, Then you shall also judge My house, And likewise have charge of My courts; I will give you places to walk among these who stand here. 'Hear, O Joshua, the high priest, you and your companions who sit before you, for they are a wondrous sign; for behold, I am bringing forth My Servant the BRANCH. For behold, the stone that I have laid before Joshua: Upon the stone are seven eyes. Behold, **I will** engrave its inscription,' Says the Lord of hosts, 'and **I will** remove the iniquity of that land in one day. In that day,' says the Lord of hosts, 'Everyone will invite his neighbor under his vine and under his fig tree."* (Zechariah 3:7-10)

WHAT ARE YOUR CIRCUMSTANCES?

Are you going through a painful time in your life? Are these circumstances tempting you to question your faith? Are you being oppressed by outside forces? Do your enemies seem too powerful for you to escape their grasp? Are you living under harsh financial circumstances? Does it seem like the mess you are in has gotten so bad that it is beyond repair? Do you sometimes feel that your situation is impossible? As you have been trying to stand in faith, have your circumstances appeared to get worse and worse each passing day?

If you are experiencing one or more of these challenges, I have some good news for you. It is in times exactly like this that the Lord speaks in power. It is in times like these that He releases His awesome "*I will*" messages to you. You need to be listening and standing in faith to receive all His wonderful promises. It is time to trust the promises and wait for the fullness of His deliverance. Again I say: Don't quit! Don't give up. Remember the powerful promise Yeshua gave in Luke 21:28, "*Now when these things begin to happen, look up and lift up your heads, because your redemption draws near.*"

YESHUA MODELS IT FOR US.

At this point, it is important to remember that the Lord is not wishy/washy. Think about what Paul is saying in 2 Corinthians 1:18-19, "*But as God is faithful, our word to you was not Yes and No. For the Son of God, Jesus Christ, who was preached among you by us—by me, Silvanus, and Timothy—was not Yes and No, but in Him was Yes."* In other words, the Lord doesn't give a promise and then take it back. He doesn't tell you all the great things He has done for others and then say "No" to you. Remember that He is the same yesterday, today, and forever (Hebrews 13:8) Paul continues this teaching in 2 Corinthians 1:20, *"For all the promises of God in Him are Yes, and in Him Amen, to the glory of God through us."* He does not say "Yes" when He means "No." All His promises are trustworthy. Yeshua is our living model for this. I like the way this is stated in the Complete Jewish Bible.

> *For however many promises God has made, they all find their "Yes" in connection with him (Yeshua); that is why it is through him that we say the "Amen" when we give glory to God.* (2 Corinthians 1:20, CJB)

Think about it. Paul said to the church in Corinth, *"For all the promises of God in Him are Yes…"* Yeshua is the promise of God. He is the great *"I will"* of God the Father. He wants to bring the full manifestation of these promises into your world. He always does it on behalf of the Father so He may receive all the glory. This is what He does and this is who He is. You can trust Him. He does not change. He will do what He has said He will do. Amen?

Remember this promise: "With God, it is always "Yes" and "Amen." This is why I believe the seven *"I will"* promises of God are for you and me. I want to repeat this over and over so that it will sink deeply into your spirit and be activated in your life. I know this is repetitious, but repetition is one of the powerful keys to learning. I practice this in my own life and ministry and I have found that my faith grows each time I speak these things aloud. Now I am asking you to do the same thing. Read the passage below again and then read it aloud again.

> *For the Son of God, Jesus Christ, who was preached among you by us—by me, Silvanus, and Timothy—was not Yes and No, but in Him was Yes. For all the promises of God in Him are Yes, and in Him Amen, to the glory of God through us.* (2 Corinthians 1:19-20)

Hold on to this thought: Yeshua is the fulfillment of all the "I will" promises of the Father for you and me. I looked this up on my computer version of the Bible. The words, *"I will"* are mentioned 1,744 times in the NKJV. Not all of them are direct promises of the Lord, but most of them are. After you master the art of praying in this new way, search for more of these promises and implement them. You can find even more of them with a computer search of the Bible. With each promise: receive it, activate it, and release its power in your life and ministry.

The best way to build a skill is through practice. In this section, I am giving you the opportunity for some practice. Consider the following three passages. Begin to accept Yeshua as the Lord's way of activating these promises. He does it and then releases us to do the same things. Remember John 14:12-14, *"Most assuredly, I say to you, he who believes in Me, the works that I do he will do also; and greater works than these he will do, because I go to My Father. And whatever you ask in My name, that I will do, that the Father may be glorified in the Son. If you ask anything in My name,* **I will do it**.*" Did you notice that Yeshua continues to release more of these "I will" promises? Think about this as you read the first of the three passages below:*

> *And behold, a leper came and worshiped Him, saying, "Lord, if You are willing, You can make me clean." Then Jesus put out His hand and touched him, saying, "***I am willing***; be cleansed." Immediately his leprosy was cleansed.* (Matthew 8:2-3)

Pause and think about this for a moment. Don't just read through it. We want to receive it and activate it. Here is a thought: Jesus was always willing. We see it over and over in the New Testament. Do you think He has changed? Has He suddenly stopped being willing to do His work through us? I don't think so. I believe this powerful promise in the Bible: "He is the same yesterday, today and forever." So prayerfully ask this question: Is He now unwilling to help people in need? What does your faith say to you? Now move on to the second passage.

> *Now when Jesus had entered Capernaum, a centurion came to Him, pleading with Him, saying, "Lord, my servant is lying at home paralyzed, dreadfully tormented." And Jesus said to him, "***I will come and heal him***."* (Matthew 8:5-7)

In this passage, we see that Jesus promises that He will do two things which the centurion had requested. He will come when you invite Him. When He comes, He will heal you. You don't have to beg. He has already answered – Yes, I will! Now pause and claim it for yourself. Then give Him praise and glory for manifesting what He has promised in your life. Remember if it doesn't happen immediately, keep confessing it until it manifests. Now move on to the third passage for your study.

*Come to Me, all you who labor and are heavy laden, and **I will give you rest**. Take My yoke upon you and learn from Me, for I am gentle and lowly in heart, and you will find rest for your souls. For My yoke is easy and My burden is light.* (Matthew 11:28-30)

Are you tired and weighed down with heavy burdens? Does everything you try to do spiritually appear to result in a big battle or a huge struggle? Does it feel like nothing is easy for you anymore? Well, I have some really good news for you! Yeshua has already said, "I will." He will give you rest when you are tired and burdened. He has already decreed that His yoke and His burden are light. Believe His promises. Receive them by faith and activate them as He is teaching you.

Think about this: The main spiritual question is not whether the Lord is willing. He made that abundantly clear long ago. The real question is about our willingness to accept the promises and to let them work in our lives and ministries. Are you ready and willing to let Him activate your faith? Are you ready to receive what He has already given? Remember, you don't have to beg. He is willing. Receive it with the spiritual gift of faith (1 Corinthians 12:9a, "…*to another faith by the same Spirit…*"). This faith is a "power gift" from the Holy Spirit which He has already given to you. Remember my challenge given above. As you become more proficient at using these gifts from the Lord, begin to embrace and activate other "*I will*" promises in the Bible.

SELAH QUESTIONS

(Selah means to pause and meditate on these things.)

1. Describe how you can activate the "I will" promises of the Lord?

_____

_____

_____

2. Have you activated the Lord's promises before? If so, how did you do that?

_____

_____

_____

3. Considering this, how would you categorize your prayers?

_____

_____

_____

4. What are your circumstances in which you need promises from the Lord?

_____

_____

_____

5. What did Paul mean when he wrote, "*For all the promises of God in Him are Yes...*"?

_____

_____

_____

6. Name some "I will" promises which have influenced your ministry.

_____

_____

_____

7. What "I will" promises have you received from Yeshua?

_____

_____

_____

8. How have you activated these promises?

_____

_____

_____

9. What difference has this made in your life and ministry?

_____

_____

_____

CHAPTER TWO

Promise One

"I Will Sprinkle Clean Water On You"

As you review the seven promises of restoration given by the Lord in the passage below from the book of Ezekiel, read them aloud and make them your own. The promises are empowered when they are spoken aloud. Then they take root in hearts that are prepared and ready to receive them anew from the Lord. As you read these promises again, stop and take steps to receive each one by faith before moving on to the next one. In the next seven chapters, we will go into greater detail about the Lord's full meaning being revealed and released in each promise. Receive them now at face value trusting that the Lord has your best interests at heart. Remember His promise in Jeremiah 29:11, "*For I know the thoughts that I think toward you, says the Lord, thoughts of peace and not of evil, to give you a future and a hope.*" This is the Lord's attitude toward you as you approach Him to receive each of His promises.

> Then *I will **sprinkle clean water** on you, and you will be clean; **I will cleanse you from all your uncleanness** and from all your idols. **I will give you a new heart** and put a new spirit within you; **I will take the stony heart out of your flesh and give you a heart of flesh. I will put My Spirit inside you** and cause you to walk in My laws, respect my rulings and obey them. You will live in the land I gave to your ancestors. You will be my people, and **I will be your God. I will save you from all your uncleanliness. I will summon the grain and increase it,** and not send famine against you. **I will multiply the yield** of fruit from the trees and increase production in the fields, so that you never again suffer the reproach of famine among the nations.* (Ezekiel 36:25-30, CJB)

In this chapter, we will begin by looking at **Promise One**. Adonai says, "*Then I will sprinkle clean water on you, and you will be clean*" (Ezekiel 36:25). In some ways, this is a symbolic washing. I see this as the Lord's answer to David's challenging questions in Psalm 24:3-4: "*Who may ascend into the hill of the Lord? Or who may stand in His holy place? He who has clean hands and a pure heart, who has not lifted up his soul to an idol, nor sworn deceitfully.*" These two questions are dealt with again in the New Testament. This time the challenge is given in the form of a directive: "*Draw near to God and He* *will draw near to you. Cleanse your hands, you sinners; and purify your hearts, you double-minded."* (James 4:8).

If you read this passage from Psalm 24 and the one from James 4 apart from the promise given in Ezekiel, it appears to be impossible to do what is spiritually needed. The good news is that Father God promised this cleansing long ago and has now fulfilled the promise through the completed work of Yeshua ha Messiach. The fulfillment of this promise is such an amazing thing and He has freely given it to you and me. We are given Yeshua's righteousness and His cleanliness as we approach the Lord. I just want to say over and over, "Thank you, Father God! Thank you, Yeshua! Hallelujah!"

The process described in Ezekiel chapter thirty-six appears to be an outward and symbolic cleansing similar to what we experience in water baptism. The Lord has done the work and we only need to receive it. We are only required to let Him do the needed spiritual work as we ceremonially consecrate ourselves to Him. In the more complete explanation given through Ezekiel (which came along much later than the revelation to Moses), we see that this is the way the Lord prepared the priests and Levites for their service in the Tabernacle and later in the Temple. What we can see in the Lord's work with Moses is that this was a complex and detailed ceremonial process. Don't worry, the real work is always done by the Lord. He does this over and over for those who faithfully seek to serve Him – for those who seek His face.

Then the Lord spoke to Moses, saying: "Take the Levites from among the children of Israel and cleanse them ceremonially. Thus you shall do to them to cleanse them: Sprinkle water of purification on them, and let them shave all their body, and let them wash their clothes, and so make themselves clean." (Numbers 8:5-7)

In the Lord's instructions to Moses, you can see more clearly the process for spiritual cleansing. This was later extended to you and me as a promise through the prophet Ezekiel. It is the Lord's plan and gift for you and me as we serve as kingdom priests. This is the idea behind the ceremonial washing which was required of each person entering the Temple for worship. They washed off in any one of the many mikvahs (place of washing) archaeologists have found throughout Israel. Each person took a mikvah (at times spelled: mikveh) dip before entering the Temple.

If you have been to Israel and seen these places of washing, you know that the water was not technically clean. The water did not flow through the mikvah and over time many things fell into the water. This form of washing one's self was not like a bath we normally take these days to make our physical bodies clean. The service of the sprinkling of water, ordered by the Lord, was used to cleanse people of many spiritual problems as well as for physical defilement. When the psalmist cried out to be clean in the Lord's eyes, he was activating the promise. *"Purge me with hyssop, and I shall be clean; wash me, and I shall be whiter than snow."* (Psalm 51:7)

And for an unclean person they shall take some of the ashes of the heifer burnt for purification from sin, and running water shall be put on them in a vessel. A clean person shall take hyssop and dip it in the water, sprinkle it on the tent, on all the vessels, on the persons who were there, or on the one who touched a bone, the slain, the dead, or a grave. The clean person shall sprinkle the unclean on the third day and on the seventh day; and on the seventh day he shall purify himself, wash his clothes, and bathe in water; and at evening he shall be clean. (Numbers 19:17-19)

One thing which is often said and is included in many liturgies for baptism is: "Water baptism is an outward and visible sign of an inward and spiritual work." This is founded on the same ideas and doctrines included in the Lord's first promise of restoration. He is letting us be spiritually restored to the human state as it was before the fall in the Garden of Eden. These experiences have always been short-lived because natural sin is still present in each of us. This knowledge keeps us humble and this process gives us the ability to be ready to access the presence and power of the Lord at any given time. James gives a more complete explanation of the process in the passage below.

Therefore submit to God. Resist the devil and he will flee from you. Draw near to God and He will draw near to you. Cleanse your hands, you sinners; and purify your hearts, you double-minded. Lament

*and mourn and weep! Let your laughter be turned
to mourning and your joy to gloom. Humble yourselves in the sight of the Lord, and He will lift you
up.* (James 4:7-10)

Each time we receive cleansing by the Lord, it opens the way
for us to receive many spiritual blessings. In this process, the
Lord does two amazing and wonderful works of grace for us.
We should always be thankful for one amazing and wonderful
thing which the Lord always does. He both cleanses us and
rewards us for being clean. When our cleansing comes from
the Lord we are enabled to access greater things. Note in the
passage below another "I will" promise of the Lord. He will
enable you to be restored so you can receive what has been
stored up for you. When I read these things over and over,
and as I speak them aloud, I want to cry out, **"Hallelujah!
The Lord is good and His mercy and love endure forever!"**
What an awesome God we serve! What an awesome Savior
who made all this possible for us! What an awesome Holy
Spirit who continues to release these things today for you
and me! Amen? Now read it aloud for yourself in the Lord's
own words:

> *Thus says the Lord God: "On the day that I cleanse
> you from all your iniquities, **I will also enable you**
> to dwell in the cities, and the ruins shall be rebuilt.
> The desolate land shall be tilled instead of lying des-
> olate in the sight of all who pass by. So they will
> say, 'This land that was desolate has become like
> the Garden of Eden; and the wasted, desolate, and*

*ruined cities are now fortified and inhabited.' Then the nations which are left all around you shall know that I, the Lord, have rebuilt the ruined places and planted what was desolate. **I, the Lord, have spoken it, and I will do it.***" (Ezekiel 36:33-36)

Look again at the promise: "*Then I will sprinkle clean water on you, and you will be clean;*" (Ezekiel 36:25) As you continue to study this promise, I remind you once again to read it aloud several times. Keep reading it until you make it your own. The promises are activated and empowered when spoken aloud as they take root in your heart. As with the others, receive this promise now at face value trusting that the Lord has your best interests at heart. Notice once again that the promise in Psalm 24:3-4 is spoken again in the New Testament in the form of a directive in James 4:8.

I want to share another challenging fact which I have discovered as I teach these lessons. Some people reject much of what I share from the Old Testament. There is a false theology circulating now which claims everything in the Old Testament is fulfilled and no longer of use for modern believers. I do not share this belief. I believe that every word of scripture is true, valuable, and eternal. Consider what Paul wrote in 2 Timothy 3:16-17, "*All Scripture is given by inspiration of God, and is profitable for doctrine, for reproof, for correction, for instruction in righteousness, that the man of God may be complete, thoroughly equipped for every good work.*" The only available scriptures when

Paul wrote this were the Torah and the other writings we now call the Old Testament. Jesus also dealt with this kind of incorrect thinking in the very strong and clear passage below.

> *Do not think that I came to destroy the Law or the Prophets. I did not come to destroy but to fulfill. For assuredly, I say to you, till heaven and earth pass away, one jot or one tittle will by no means pass from the law till all is fulfilled. Whoever therefore breaks one of the least of these commandments, and teaches men so, shall be called least in the kingdom of heaven; but whoever does and teaches them, he shall be called great in the kingdom of heaven.* (Matthew 5:17-19)

In the passage above, the Complete Jewish Bible translates all the references to the law as "Torah". The primary definition of the word Torah is teaching. In this case the teachings of God. These do not change with time or by popular human thought. According to Yeshua, we will be held accountable for how we handle the Torah of God. Whoever rejects the teachings of the Lord and teaches others to do so will be called least in the kingdom of heaven. I see two very important lessons in the words of Yeshua. The first and most obvious is that the Word of God does not expire. The second thing is a reminder to me that His promises are as relevant today as when He first released them.

MISSION IMPOSSIBLE

Think about it! It seems impossible to do what is spiritually needed in this process of receiving and activating the Lord's promise. The good news is that the Lord promised this cleansing long ago and He kept the promise to that generation. Much later He fulfilled the promise again through the life and work of Yeshua. In this work of Yeshua, we are spiritually given His righteousness and His cleanliness as we approach the Lord. This is similar to what we experience in water baptism. The Lord has done the work and we only need to jump in and receive it.

This cleansing by the Lord opens the way for many spiritual blessings. I want to speak of two blessings once again both for clarity and to help us remember them. The Lord does two amazing and wonderful works of grace for us in this process. He both cleanses us and rewards us for being clean. He does the work and rewards us for allowing Him to do it. That is truly amazing grace. In the section below, I want to go through this process in greater detail. I want you to understand more of the fullness of what the Lord has done for you in the past as well as what He is still doing for you in the present. What you cannot do for yourself, He is willing and able to do for you. It is time to believe the promise. It is time to receive it and activate it in your spirit.

YESHUA CLARIFIED THE PROCESS

*Blind Pharisee, first cleanse the inside of the cup
and dish, that the outside of them may be clean also.*
(Matthew 23:26)

Jesus is saying that it is our responsibility to cleanse ourselves. As you reflect on how you can do this, it seems impossible for us to accomplish this on our own. Paul's teaching in Second Corinthians reaffirms this issue of our responsibility for getting clean and staying clean. "*Therefore, having these promises, beloved, let us cleanse ourselves from all filthiness of the flesh and spirit, perfecting holiness in the fear of God.*" (2 Corinthians 7:1). Even though Yeshua does all of the work, it is still fundamentally our responsibility. Let this be clear. The Lord is not excusing us from our responsibility. He is providing a way for it to be possible. The good news is that the Lord has done the work for us and, all we need to do is receive it and activate it.

As I continued to study the process of cleansing, I noticed that the Bible identifies three ways this can be accomplished. In the spiritual realm, the Word of God is viewed as living water which has the power to sprinkle and make us clean. This is made clear in Ephesians 5:25b-26, "*Christ also loved the church and gave Himself for her, that He might sanctify and cleanse her with the washing of water by the word,*" His love and grace make the impossible possible for us. Think about what the Lord is saying. The Word of God is living water that can cleanse us. Every time you read these things aloud think about that and continuously give Him your gratitude and praise. Amen?

The second method I found for activating the promises is through the sacrificial blood of Jesus. It is Yeshua's blood which cleanses our conscience, sets us free from the dead works of the flesh, and enables us to serve the living God through living works. This sounds complex and many people struggle to understand it. Here is a unique thought: you don't have to understand it fully. You only need to receive it and activate it in your spiritual life. Thank you, Yeshua! In the passage below, the writer of the book of Hebrews gives you a working definition of this process. As you read it aloud, once again receive it and activate it in your heart. Amen?

> For if the blood of bulls and goats and the ashes of a heifer, sprinkling the unclean, sanctifies for the purifying of the flesh, how much more shall the blood of Christ, who through the eternal Spirit offered Himself without spot to God, cleanse your conscience from dead works to serve the living God? (Hebrews 9:13-14)

The third method of Biblical cleansing is found in 1 John 1:9, "If we confess our sins, He is faithful and just to forgive us our sins and to cleanse us from all unrighteousness." Through the act of repentance, our sins are forgiven. Once the sins are forgiven we are then cleansed by the Lord from all unrighteousness. In addition to the teaching of the Torah, this cleansing was also mandated through the Prophet Isaiah. In the passages below the Lord makes it clear that we are to keep ourselves spiritu-ally clean. We must stop touching the unclean things of the flesh in spirit, soul, or body. Like the audience addressed by Isaiah, we are tasked to carry the vessels of the Lord. Those who love and obey Yeshua ha Messiach are the temples of God and His Holy presence is carried in our hearts (spirit). We must keep His temple within us spiritually clean. Amen?

> *Depart! Depart! Go out from there, touch no unclean thing; go out from the midst of her, be clean, you who bear the vessels of the Lord. For you shall not go out with haste, nor go by flight; for the Lord will go before you, and the God of Israel will be your rear guard.* (Isaiah 52:11-12)

> *And you shall take some of the blood that is on the altar, and some of the anointing oil, and sprinkle it on Aaron and on his garments, on his sons and on the garments of his sons with him; and he and his garments shall be hallowed, and his sons and his sons' garments with him.* (Exodus 29:21)

LEARNING TO REMEMBER

When this thought came to me by the Holy Spirit, it sounded strange. I had to reflect on it for a long time. My question was, "Is remembering a learned process?" I came to understand that it is and many have not yet learned the lesson. In the first book in this series entitled *"REDEMPTION,"* I pointed out that the Lord had given some powerful and visual means for the people to remember His "I will" promises. He did this through teachings included in the Passover Haggadah (The Telling). The four cups of wine and the words associated with them were clear reminders to be considered by all believers at least once a year. Some Hebrew scholars also believe that the four corners of the Prayer Shawl with the tassels were also reminders of the four main promises of redemption. In the Torah, the Lord instructed them to wear the prayer shawl with tassels tied on all four corners. In the same passage of scripture, the Lord said this was done so they would remember that He had rescued them from Egypt.

In the same way, the Lord gave the Hebrew people the mikvah ritual as a means of constant remembrance. They were required to do this before entering the Temple. Each time they went through the mikvah, they remembered that the Lord was cleansing them. For us, we are invited to remember in Christian baptism. Not only in our baptism but each time we witness the baptism of others who are being added to the body of believers. Each time, we are reminded that it is the Lord who cleanses us thereby enabling us to access His gifts and grace.

PRAYER

Purge me with hyssop, and I shall be clean; wash me, and I shall be whiter than snow. Make me hear joy and gladness, that the bones You have broken may rejoice. Hide Your face from my

sins, and blot out all my iniquities. Create in me a clean heart,
O God, and renew a steadfast spirit within me. Do not cast me
away from Your presence, and do not take Your Holy Spirit
from me. Restore to me the joy of Your salvation, and uphold
me by Your generous Spirit. Then I will teach transgressors Your
ways, and sinners shall be converted to You. (Psalm 51:7-13)

REINFORCEMENT TRAINING

In the passages of scripture below, prayerfully study them and
let the Holy Spirit teach you the profound meaning in each.
Consider how important this is to the Lord. If for no other
reason, we should do it simply to please Him. Remember
that He is more pleased with obedience than sacrifice. I consider each of these passages to be an integral part of rein-
forcing these principles in our relationship with the Lord.
This spiritual discipline is one of the keys to seeking His face
and becoming part of the generation that walks in intimacy
with the Lord.

> *Then the Lord spoke to Moses, saying: "Take the*
> *Levites from among the children of Israel and*
> *cleanse them ceremonially. Thus you shall do to*
> *them to cleanse them: Sprinkle water of purifica-*
> *tion on them, and let them shave all their body, and*
> *let them wash their clothes, and so make them-*
> *selves clean. Then let them take a young bull with*
> *its grain offering of fine flour mixed with oil, and*
> *you shall take another young bull as a sin offering.*

And you shall bring the Levites before the tabernacle of meeting, and you shall gather together the whole congregation of the children of Israel. So you shall bring the Levites before the Lord, and the children of Israel shall lay their hands on the Levites; and Aaron shall offer the Levites before the Lord like a wave offering from the children of Israel, that they may perform the work of the Lord. Then the Levites shall lay their hands on the heads of the young bulls, and you shall offer one as a sin offering and the other as a burnt offering to the Lord, to make atonement for the Levites. (Numbers 8:5-12)

And I commanded the Levites that they should cleanse themselves, and that they should go and guard the gates, to sanctify the Sabbath day. (Nehemiah 13:22)

Wash me thoroughly from my iniquity, and cleanse me from my sin. (Psalm51:2)

How can a young man cleanse his way? By taking heed according to Your word. With my whole heart I have sought You; Oh, let me not wander from Your commandments! Your word I have hidden in my heart, That I might not sin against You. (Psalm 119:9-11)

They shall not defile themselves anymore with their idols, nor with their detestable things, nor with any of their transgressions; but I will deliver them from all their dwelling places in which they have sinned, and will cleanse them. Then they shall be My people, and I will be their God. (Ezekiel 37:23)

THE MISSION IS NOW OURS

Many people are content thinking that Yeshua became flesh and worked all these amazing things for us. They are content as long as it places no claim on their lives and service. The challenge comes when they are asked to do what Jesus did. They are not secure with the idea that they are to carry on this awesome work of God. As I reflected on this, I remembered two things Yeshua said. In John 9:5, it is recorded that Yeshua proclaimed: "*As long as I am in the world, I am the light of the world.*" This is widely accepted by the people we are discussing here as long as we do not bring up Yeshua's words found in the Gospel of Matthew.

You are the light of the world. A city that is set on a hill cannot be hidden. Nor do they light a lamp and put it under a basket, but on a lampstand, and it gives light to all who are in the house. Let your light so shine before men, that they may see your good works and glorify your Father in heaven. (Matthew 5:14-16)

How about you? Are you ready, willing, and able to carry on the work of Christ in your generation? Yeshua has already equipped you for the task. Remember His words in John 14:12, *"Most assuredly, I say to you, he who believes in Me, the works that I do he will do also; and greater works than these he will do because I go to My Father.* If you truly believe in Yeshua, you will do the works He did during His ministry on the Earth. You will have the opportunity, blessing, anointing, and power to do *"greater works than these."* How can we possibly do greater works than Yeshua did in His generation? Yeshua didn't ask us to think about it. He gave us the command "GO." There is no maybe or perhaps later when it is convenient given in this command of the Lord. Study it again in the passage below.

> *And He said to them, "__Go__ into all the world and preach the gospel to every creature. He who believes and is baptized will be saved; but he who does not believe will be condemned. And these signs will follow those who believe: In My name they will cast out demons; they will speak with new tongues; they will take up serpents; and if they drink anything deadly, it will by no means hurt them; they will lay hands on the sick, and they will recover."* (Mark 16:15-18)

This sending forth to do His work was a part of Yeshua's apostolic training program. He first sent twelve disciples with instructions on their assigned work. He said to them what He is saying to you "GO." It will never be easy. It wasn't easy for them and it will not be easy for you and me, but it is our mission. It is our destiny in the Kingdom of God. You can see this clearly in Yeshua's instruction in the passage below. I highlighted parts for emphasis. I especially like His words: "*Freely you have received, freely give.*" I also highlighted the task to "*cleanse the lepers.*" Freely He has cleansed us by the washing of the word and we are to freely cleanse all who need it in the world around us.

> *These twelve Jesus sent out and commanded them, saying: "Do not go into the way of the Gentiles, and do not enter a city of the Samaritans. But* **go** *rather to the lost sheep of the house of Israel. And as you go, preach, saying, 'The kingdom of heaven is at hand.' Heal the sick,* **cleanse the lepers***, raise the dead, cast out demons.* **Freely you have received, freely give***. Provide neither gold nor silver nor copper in your money belts, nor bag for your journey, nor two tunics, nor sandals, nor staffs; for a worker is worthy of his food.* (Matthew 10:5-10)

The handoff has been made. The mission is yours and mine. Now it is time for us to hear the word of the Lord telling us to "GO." In the passage below notice that there are more promises given to those who accept the Lord's calling and commissioning. Your prayers will be answered. When you walk in unity with others, you open the floodgates of Heaven so that more blessings than you can contain will flow to you and through you. What an honor and privilege to be part of Yeshua's work bringing glory to the Father!

Most assuredly, I say to you, he who believes in Me, the works that I do he will do also; and greater works than these he will do, because I go to My Father. And whatever you ask in My name, that I will do, that the Father may be glorified in the Son. If you ask anything in My name, I will do it. (John 14:12-14)

ACTIVATION

Are you ready to make some powerful spiritual "I will" promises to the Lord? Remember that this is one of the things David did to activate the Lord's promises in his life and service for the Kingdom. The prophet Micah also did this in his relationship with the Lord. Micah saw the Lord's salvation before it manifested in his generation. He claimed the outcomes of the vision and positioned himself to receive all the promises the Lord had made for repentant remnants of His people. Think about this as you read aloud the passage below. Then activate the promises in your life and work.

*But as for me, **I will** look to Adonai; **I will** wait for the God of my salvation; my God will hear me. Enemies of mine, don't gloat over me! Although I have fallen, **I will** rise; though I live in the dark, Adonai is my light. **I will** endure Adonai's rage, because I sinned against Him, until He pleads my cause and judges in my favor. Then he will bring me out to the light; and **I will** see His justice. My enemies will see it too, and* *shame will cover those who said to me, "Where is Adonai your God?"* **I will** *gloat over them, as they are trampled underfoot like mud in the streets.* (Micah 7:7-10, CJB)

JACOB'S ACTIVATION PRAYER

The process of activation has been exercised throughout the generations of those who seek the Lord. In the passage below, you see Jacob doing these same things long before they occurred to David. Read Jacob's words aloud and claim the Lord's promises for your life. The last verse clearly states the promise for Jacob and his family. Do you believe the promise is also for you? If so, receive it and activate it now.

Then Jacob said, "O God of my father Abraham and God of my father Isaac, the Lord who said to me, 'Return to your country and to your family, and I will deal well with you': I am not worthy of the least of all the mercies and of all the truth which You have shown Your servant; for I crossed over this Jordan with my staff, and now I have become two companies. Deliver me, I pray, from the hand of my brother, from the hand of Esau; for I fear him, lest he come and attack me and the mother with the children. For You said, 'I will surely treat you well, and make your descendants as the sand of the sea, which cannot be numbered for multitude.'" (Genesis 32:9-12)

SELAH QUESTIONS

(Selah means to pause and meditate on these things.)

1. Have you received this promised cleansing from the Lord?

_____

_____

_____

2. If not, what steps should you take to receive it?

_____

_____

_____

3. How can you assist others in this amazing cleansing of the Lord?

_____

_____

_____

4. When something seems impossible where do you turn for help?

_____

_____

_____

5. How did Yeshua clarify this for us?

_____

_____

_____

6. Has Yeshua sent you to do His work in this generation?

_____

_____

_____

7. If so, how are you making it happen for the Glory of the Father?

_____

_____

_____

CHAPTER THREE

Promise Two

"I Will Cleanse You"

I will cleanse you from all your uncleanness and from all your idols. (Ezekiel 36:25a)

This promise of the Lord speaks directly to the inward process of spiritual cleansing. In the New Testament, we know this as Holy Spirit Baptism. The water baptism we looked at in the previous chapter only cleanses the outside. Holy Spirit baptism cleanses the inside. John, the baptizer, shared his testimony as a means of releasing this amazing gift from God. You can find his testimony in John 1:33-34, "*I did not know Him, but He who sent me to baptize with water said to me, 'Upon whom you see the Spirit descending, and remaining on Him, this is He who baptizes with the Holy Spirit.' And I have seen and testified that this is the Son of God.*"

The release of this promise did not come as a sudden, unexpected, or isolated event. It had been prophesied long ago.

This promise had been requested in prayer for centuries dating back at least to the beginning of the exodus from Egypt. This was the fulfillment of a prophetic prayer given by Moses in Numbers 11:29, "*Then Moses said to him, "Are you zealous for my sake? Oh, that all the Lord's people were prophets and that the Lord would put His Spirit upon them!"* Moses asked for all the Children of Israel to receive the Holy Spirit. This was also the prayer of David lifted up to Father God when he was confronted with his uncleanness before the Lord. As David repented of his sin, he cried out, "*Wash me thoroughly from my iniquity, and cleanse me from my sin.*" (Psalm 51:2)

Perhaps you have gone through a time of deep repentance – a time when you felt unclean because of something you said, something you did or something you left undone. At times like these, the only hope is that the Lord will move once again to cleanse you from within. Perhaps you have looked at John's ministry of repentance and celebrated the great truth he released to those seeking the Lord that day. "*I indeed baptize you with water unto repentance, but He who is coming after me is mightier than I, whose sandals I am not worthy to carry. He will baptize you with the Holy Spirit and fire.* (Matthew 3:11)

Some texts leave out the two powerful words "and fire." I like the imagery of fire in this instance. I believe the Lord wants to cleanse us and burn away all the evidence that our guilty actions ever took place. To me, it is a visual image of what the Lord said in Jeremiah 31:34b, "*For I will forgive their iniquity, and their sin I will remember no more.*" It is important to always remember that water baptism is an outward and visible sign of an inward and spiritual work.

> *But the Holy Spirit also witnesses to us; for after He had said before, "This is the covenant that I will make with them after those days, says the LORD: I will put My laws into their hearts, and in their minds I will write them," then He adds, "Their sins and their lawless deeds I will remember no more." Now where there is remission of these, there is no longer an offering for sin.* (Hebrews 10:15-18)

The Lord does the inward and spiritual work. What an amazing and wonderful thought that He would do that for us. I am always in awe as I consider what the Lord has promised. I am so thankful that He always keeps His promises. Consider how important this promise is for our spiritual wellbeing: *"If we confess our sins, He is faithful and just to forgive us our sins and to cleanse us from all unrighteousness."* (1 John 1:9) He doesn't do a partial work in us and expect us to fill in all the rest. He does it all. He cleanses us from all unrighteousness. Thanks be to our God and Father and the Lord Yeshua ha Messiach! All we have to do is believe it, receive it, and activate it.

"I Will Cleanse You"

> *Woe to you, scribes and Pharisees, hypocrites! For you cleanse the outside of the cup and dish, but*

inside they are full of extortion and self-indulgence.
Blind Pharisee, first cleanse the inside of the cup
and dish, that the outside of them may be clean also.
(Matthew 23:25-26)

Many people who profess that they are religious appear to only work hard to look righteous in the eyes of other people. This was true in Yeshua's time as it is in ours. People who are controlled by a religious spirit (the modern version of Pharisees and Scribes) work to make their outer appearance look as if it is clean while they remain unclean in their hearts and minds. A little outward cleansing is all they are doing. The real need is for us to let this work of the Lord come into our hearts as we let Him do a thorough job of cleansing our spirits. The problem here is that many people have no idea how to do that.

Remember from the last chapter that water baptism is an outward and visible sign of an inward and spiritual blessing. Some people do the outward sign but neglect the inward and spiritual part of their lives. A simple fact in the spiritual realm is that people can't cleanse their hearts. This is done by the work of God. This is the purpose of the second "I will" promise of the Lord given through Ezekiel. The Lord said, "*I will cleanse you from all your uncleanness and from all your idols.*" (Ezekiel 36:25a) This speaks of an inward process of cleansing. As I stated above, this is often called "Holy Spirit Baptism." Consider again what David did when his sin became publicly known, he cried out to the Lord, "*Wash me thoroughly from my iniquity, and cleanse me from my sin."* (Psalm 51:2)

As David reflected on his relationship with the Lord, he wrote the beautiful psalm below for those who are committed to drawing closer to the Lord. David refers to them as those who seek the Lord's face. I like to believe that I am in this same generation of seekers – *"This is Jacob, the generation of those who seek Him..."* How about you? Are you seeking the Lord? Are you seeking His face? Do you hunger and thirst for Him? How can we ever be clean enough to be in His presence? This is the question which David is wrestling through in the passage below.

> *Who may ascend into the hill of the Lord? Or who may stand in His holy place? He who has clean hands and a pure heart, who has not lifted up his soul to an idol, nor sworn deceitfully. He shall receive blessing from the Lord, and righteousness from the God of his salvation. This is Jacob, the generation of those who seek Him, who seek Your face.* (Psalm 24:3-6)

David recognized that some of his faults were even hidden from him. It is the same for us. Some of our sins are so secret that we are not able to see them. We need help from someone else to make them clear to us. The problem is that most people do not like to have their shortcomings pointed out by another person. This is the reason David and others have always gone to the Lord for help. We ask the Lord to open our spiritual eyes so we can see these hidden spiritual truths. We cry out with David for the Lord to cleanse us from "secret faults" and from "presumptuous sins." David realized this was the only way he would ever be able to be spiritually clean enough to be in the Lord's presence. It is time to look at ourselves and call to the Lord to make us aware of our secret faults and then to be wise enough to allow Him to make us clean.

> *Who can understand his errors? Cleanse me from secret faults. Keep back Your servant also from presumptuous sins; let them not have dominion over me. Then I shall be blameless, and I shall be innocent of great transgression.* (Psalm 19:12-13)

Give thanks to the Lord. He has already established a process for us to get clean in our inward being. I asked you to look at this scripture earlier to share the heart cry of David for inner cleansing. Now, look at it as an example of how to let these things manifest in your heart. Remember that in his first epistle, John made the process clear for us to see. "*If we confess our sins, He is faithful and just to forgive us our sins and to cleanse us from all unrighteousness.*" (1 John 1:9) The really good news is that the Lord is both willing and faithful. We can trust Him to cleanse us if we truly repent. The reason John points to the fact that the Lord is "just" is that He is always faithful to keep His promises. Consider the promise of the Lord again: "*I will cleanse you from all your uncleanness and from all your idols.*" (Ezekiel 36:25a)

I want to point out one very special word in this passage from Ezekiel. The word is "all." It is the same truth spoken by John in His first book. It sounds simple, but some people have difficulty believing this word. They immediately begin to reason it down "to most", but this is not what the Lord said. He said, "all." Others take it further and reduce it to a promise which "sometimes" may happen. It always amazes me how hard some people work to reduce the power of the Lord's promises in their lives. It is so important to believe the fullness of what the Lord promises if you desire to receive all the Lord has for you Then remember that the Bible says over and over that all things are possible with the Lord. Amen?

> *For if the blood of bulls and goats and the ashes of a heifer, sprinkling the unclean, sanctifies for the purifying of the flesh, how much more shall the blood of Christ, who through the eternal Spirit offered Himself without spot to God, cleanse your conscience from dead works to serve the living God?* (Hebrews 9:13-14)

Yeshua makes all the difference in the world. He took what was temporary and made it eternal. He took what was partial and made it complete. The Lord then gave us a powerful living parable to help us remember what He has done and is doing for us. You can find this parable is in the passage below from the book of Ephesians. You will see that this is another one of the powerful reasons why we should protect the sanctity of the marriage relationship. In this critically important relationship, we are enabled to more clearly see the nature of our relationship with the Lord.

Husbands, love your wives, just as Christ also loved the church and gave Himself for her, that He might sanctify and cleanse her with the washing of water by the word, that He might present her to Himself a glorious church, not having spot or wrinkle or any such thing, but that she should be holy and without blemish. (Ephesians 5:25-27)

YOM KIPPUR — DAY OF ATONEMENT

This shall be a statute forever for you: In the seventh month, on the tenth day of the month, you shall afflict your souls, and do no work at all, whether a native of your own country or a stranger who dwells among you. For on that day the priest shall make atonement for you, to cleanse you, that you may be clean from all your sins before the Lord. It is a sabbath of solemn rest for you, and you shall afflict your souls. It is a statute forever. (Leviticus 16:29-31)

From the beginning of His relationship with the descendants of Abraham, Isaac, and Jacob the Lord planned to make them (both as individuals and collectively) *"holy and without blemish."* In the "Appointed Times" established by the Lord during the Exodus of the Children of Israel from Egypt, He provided times, seasons, and procedures for the people and the nation to be cleansed. It quickly became clear that this was not a one-time process. Each time they were cleansed they soon behaved in ways which resulted in the loss of their spiritually clean status. At one point, frustrated by his behavior and that of the nation, Solomon cried out in Proverbs 20:9, "*Who can say, 'I have made my heart clean, I am pure from my sin'*"? Solomon understood the need to be *holy and without blemish,* but he found it impossible for him or anyone else to do it on their own.

From time to time the Lord brought judgment on the people because they had lapsed again into an unholy and unclean state. Even though the nation was justly held accountable for their periodic lapses into idolatry, grumbling, rebellion, and sin, the Lord had already devised a plan for a more permanent solution to their recurring need for another spiritual cleansing. In the primary passage of scripture we are using for this study, Father God spoke to the people once again. This time the Lord was reaching out through the prophet Ezekiel: "*Then I will sprinkle clean water on you, and you shall be clean; I will cleanse you from all your filthiness and from all your idols.*" (Ezekiel 36-25) The perfect solution didn't manifest right away. They had to wait for the Lord's timing as He released a perfect method of cleansing through the life and work of Yeshua ha Messiach.

> *I will cleanse them from all their iniquity by which they have sinned against Me, and I will pardon all their iniquities by which they have sinned and by which they have transgressed against Me. Then it shall be to Me a name of joy, a praise, and an honor before all nations of the earth, who shall hear all the good that I do to them; they shall fear and tremble*

for all the goodness and all the prosperity that I pro-
vide for it.' (Jeremiah 33:8-9)

Yom Kippur (Day of Atonement) was the interim method the
Lord devised for keeping His people cleansed. Once a year the
Lord took them through a deep cleansing process. In many
ways, we can look at Yom Kippur as a living parable the Lord
has given to help us understand that He and He alone can
fully cleanse us. *"Consecrate yourselves and be holy, because*
I am the Lord your God. Keep my decrees and follow them. I
am the Lord, who makes you holy." (Leviticus 20:7-8, NIV) We
also see in this annual remembrance that He is willing and
able to keep all His promises for us.

In the three passages below, see how the Lord reveals His
message and releases His promises in various ways and for
a variety of generations. We have these promises from the
Lord. We don't have to beg for them or do some great work
to receive them. They are freely given to us as an amazing act
of His grace. Receive these promised blessings. Activate them
in your life and ministry. Give Him praise and glory until they
manifest fully in your life. Amen?

> *Therefore, having these promises, beloved, let us*
> *cleanse ourselves from all filthiness of the flesh and*
> *spirit, perfecting holiness in the fear of God.* (2
> Corinthians 7:1)

> *How can a young man cleanse his way? By taking heed*
> *according to Your word. With my whole heart I have*

sought You; oh, let me not wander from Your commandments! Your word I have hidden in my heart, that I might not sin against You. (Psalm 119:9-11)

Who can understand his errors? Cleanse me from secret faults. Keep back Your servant also from presumptuous sins; let them not have dominion over me. Then I shall be blameless, and I shall be innocent of great transgression. Let the words of my mouth and the meditation of my heart be acceptable in Your sight, O LORD, my strength and my Redeemer. (Psalm 19:12-14)

PRAYER

Purge me with hyssop, and I shall be clean; wash me, and I shall be whiter than snow. Make me hear joy and gladness, that the bones You have broken may rejoice. Hide Your face from my sins, and blot out all my iniquities. Create in me a clean heart, O God, and renew a steadfast spirit within me. Do not cast me away from Your presence, and do not take Your Holy Spirit from me. Restore to me the joy of Your salvation, and uphold me by Your generous Spirit. Then I will teach transgressors Your ways, and sinners shall be converted to You. (Psalm 51:7-13)

MINISTRY TIME — HEALING

When we do conferences, we always pause at the end of the teaching period to minister to the people. This is often done in the form of a time of healing ministry. At this point, it occurred to me that we can do this in the lessons of this book. Our situation does not limit what the Lord can do. The healing gifts of the Holy Spirit are not limited by the context of the teaching. I am believing for you to receive healing as you go through this section of the book. Will you stand in agreement with me for your healing?

Remember at the beginning I asked you to meditate on Isaiah 57:18, "*I have seen his ways, and **will** heal him; **I will** also lead him, and **restore** comforts to him and to his mourners.*" We do not trick or mislead the Lord into believing we are clean when we are not. He knows all about us and loves us anyway. From the beginning, He is aware of all our ways: good and bad. Despite having this knowledge, He chooses to bless us, cleanse us, and release all these amazing and wonderful promises to us. I have provided several scriptures revealing the ways the Lord chooses to heal His people.

In your mind realize that time and distance do not limit a move of God. You can receive the healing you need with no human being needed as an intermediary. Trust the Word of God. Believe all His promises for you are yes and amen. Read each passage below and release the power of God already present in His Word and through His promises. Now receive and activate these additional promises of healing. Remember to read them aloud over and over until they take root in your heart.

> So you shall serve the Lord your God, and He will bless your bread and your water. And **I will** take sickness away from the midst of you. No one shall suffer miscarriage or be barren in your land; **I will** fulfill the number of your days. (Exodus 23:25-26)

> If you diligently heed the voice of the LORD your God and do what is right in His sight, give ear to His commandments and keep all His statutes, **I will** put **none of the diseases** on you which I have brought on the Egyptians. For **I am the LORD who heals you**. (Exodus 15:26)

> Return and tell Hezekiah the leader of My people, "Thus says the LORD, the God of David your father: 'I **have heard** your prayer, **I have seen** your tears; surely **I will** heal you. On the third day you shall go up to the house of the LORD'". (2 Kings 20:5)

> For **I will** restore health to you and heal you of your wounds,' says the LORD, (Jeremiah 30:17)

> Now when Jesus had entered Capernaum, a centurion came to Him, pleading with Him, saying, "Lord, my servant is lying at home paralyzed, dreadfully tormented." And Jesus said to him, "**I will** come and **heal him**." (Matthew 8:5-7)

Did you receive your healing? If not, do it again. I believe the Lord can and will keep all His promises. I believe He loves you and wants you to be well and fully functional for His kingdom work. I believe He is the healer and does not need anyone to do it for Him. At times He uses someone to work with Him in the process, but it is not needed. Trust the Lord. He wants what is best for you. Believe it. Receive it. Activate it the Biblical way. Then spend time giving Him praise and glory, even if it has not manifested yet. I believe that it will manifest. Amen?

CLEANSING FOR A PURPOSE

You cannot effectively clean a dirty floor with a filthy mop. You need to rinse it out until it is clean enough to do the work. It is the same with us. The Lord has chosen you to do a mighty work for the kingdom and He needs to cleanse you first so you can accomplish His purpose. It takes pressure, muscle, and struggle to squeeze out a wet mop. It may take a little time and divine squeezing to get the unclean things out of your life. Don't hesitate. Begin now to let the Lord prepare you for your destiny. The passage below is a little long, but it illustrates the Lord's commitment to both ceremonial and spiritual cleansing for those who serve Him.

> *Then the LORD spoke to Moses, saying: "Take the Levites from among the children of Israel and cleanse them ceremonially. Thus you shall do to them to cleanse them: Sprinkle water of purification*

on them, and let them shave all their body, and let them wash their clothes, and so make themselves clean. Then let them take a young bull with its grain offering of fine flour mixed with oil, and you shall take another young bull as a sin offering. And you shall bring the Levites before the tabernacle of meeting, and you shall gather together the whole congregation of the children of Israel. So you shall bring the Levites before the Lord, and the children of Israel shall lay their hands on the Levites; and Aaron shall offer the Levites before the Lord like a wave offering from the children of Israel, that they may perform the work of the Lord. Then the Levites shall lay their hands on the heads of the young bulls, and you shall offer one as a sin offering and the other as a burnt offering to the Lord, to make atonement for the Levites. (Numbers 8:5-12)

Much later, one of the Lord's chosen servants demonstrated that he fully understood the need for those who serve the Lord at any level to be cleansed for the task. In the passage below, notice that Nehemiah commanded the Levites who were to guard the city gates to go through the ritual cleansing before doing their jobs. Their jobs seem rather mundane for this degree of cleansing. Their task was to guard the gates so that no one would violate the Sabbath by entering or leaving to do commerce on Shabbat. Nehemiah wanted those who accepted the task to be cleansed as a means of sanctifying that special day. As I reflected on this, I wondered in my mind what it would be like if modern-day servants of the Lord were as focused on the sanctity of the work assigned to them by the Lord.

> *And I commanded the Levites that they should cleanse themselves, and that they should go and guard the gates, to sanctify the Sabbath day.* (Nehemiah 13:22)

The psalmist pondered an important question in Psalm 119. In the first two verses, he referred to the character of those who are truly blessed by the Lord. He wrote: "*Blessed are the undefiled in the way, who walk in the law of the Lord! Blessed are those who keep His testimonies, who seek Him with the whole heart!*" (Psalm 119:1-2) I want to be blessed by the Lord in this way. How about you? How do we prepare ourselves to receive what the Lord intends to give to us? In the passage below, the Psalmist is pondering this question, and then he finds his answer. The Lord has provided the answer and we can find it in His word. Obedience is the key.

> *How can a young man cleanse his way? By taking heed according to Your word. With my whole heart I have sought You; Oh, let me not wander from Your commandments! Your word I have hidden in my heart, that I might not sin against You.* (Psalm 119:9-11)

The ultimate answer is that our cleansing is from the Lord. The good news is that He has promised to do this for us. The Lord has a plan for a permanent and not just a temporary solution. He released the promise through Ezekiel in a time when this solution had not yet manifested. What the Lord promised would be perfected through the work of Yeshua ha Messiach. Since we know more of the story than what was known in the days of Ezekiel, we can fully understand that the Lord already had a plan which would be released when the time was right. Now is the time of our salvation and today is the day of our visitation. Make the Lord the cornerstone of your salvation and the source of your cleansing. Amen?

> *They shall not defile themselves anymore with their idols, nor with their detestable things, nor with any of their transgressions; but I will deliver them from all their dwelling places in which they have sinned, and will cleanse them. Then they shall be My people, and I will be their God.* (Ezekiel 37:23)

THE MISSION IS NOW OURS

During a major sports event, one of the very special moments occurs when the quarterback makes a near-perfect handoff to a runner who is then enabled to score a touchdown. These moments seem easy and smooth to the audience, but are the result of many long hours of learning and practicing each part of the process. Yeshua taught His disciples slowly and step by step for a long time. Now it was time for them to enter the game and show what they had learned. It is always a little unsettling when the coach sends you into the big game for the first time. I can only imagine how much the disciples felt challenged when the Lord sent them into the mission field. Imagine how you would feel if the Lord gave you the same commands today? Here is something for you to think about. He has already sent you. Now it is your turn.

> *These twelve Jesus sent out and commanded them, saying: "Do not go into the way of the Gentiles, and do not enter a city of the Samaritans. But go rather to the lost sheep of the house of Israel. And as you go, preach, saying, 'The kingdom of heaven is at hand.' Heal the sick, cleanse the lepers, raise the dead, cast out demons. Freely you have received, freely give. Provide neither gold nor silver nor copper in your money belts, nor bag for your journey, nor two tunics, nor sandals, nor staffs; for a worker is worthy of his food.* (Matthew 10:5-10)

When the Lord completes your training and sends you in to your portion of the harvest, He asks you for total commitment. He came with the full knowledge that He would pay the ultimate price in completing the mission He was given by the Father. The Apostle Paul was also fully aware of this when he was sent to the gentile world. He compared this to a committed husband who loves his wife enough to die for her. It is this commitment and devotion which the Lord uses to bring about the cleansing of the church. Are you up to the challenge? It is your turn now to love with the kind of love Yeshua had for you when He went to the cross. This is also the means by which the Father has cleansed us.

*Husbands, love your wives, just as Christ also loved
the church and gave Himself for her, that He might
sanctify and cleanse her with the washing of water
by the word, that He might present her to Himself a
glorious church, not having spot or wrinkle or any
such thing, but that she should be holy and without
blemish.* (Ephesians 5:25-27)

In the passage below, we are challenged to understand how
powerful and complete the Lord's process of cleansing was
made possible through the death and resurrection of Yeshua.
The writer of Hebrews ponders a powerful question. If the
blood of bulls and goats can cleanse, how much more can
the blood of Yeshua purify and cleanse us? Through Him, we
can also receive this promise of an eternal inheritance. His
cleansing is so powerful that it produces spiritual purity in
spirit, soul, and body.

*For if the blood of bulls and goats and the ashes of a
heifer, sprinkling the unclean, sanctifies for the puri-
fying of the flesh, how much more shall the blood
of Christ, who through the eternal Spirit offered
Himself without spot to God, cleanse your conscience from dead works to serve the living God?
And for this reason He is the Mediator of the new
covenant, by means of death, for the redemption
of the transgressions under the first covenant, that
those who are called may receive the promise of the
eternal inheritance.* (Hebrews 9:13-15)

How can you and I receive all the Lord has promised? He has made it so simple for us. Yet many people today miss this awesome offer of cleansing because they choose not to do what it takes. The Lord has made it simple, but it often appears to be too far away for them to fully grasp it. Don't let this happen to you. This is your moment of decision. This is the time to open your heart and let the Lord do all these powerful things in your life. Many who read this have already taken the steps to make all these promises their own, but some have not. Don't wait any longer. Do it right now. Accept Yeshua as your Lord and Savior. Then let Him activate all the promises in your life. Begin with confession and repentance in the way John explains the process to us in this passage. In this way, you will make the all-important move toward Him which will activate His promise. It is so simple. Do it now.

> *If we confess our sins, He is faithful and just to forgive us our sins and to cleanse us from all unrighteousness.* (1 John 1:9)

ACTIVATION

Paul also had some advice for his readers about how to activate the Lord's promises in their lives. First, it is critically important to know and understand the promises. You can't activate something you don't know you have. Next, Paul advises us to purify ourselves, and this is exactly what we have been studying in this chapter. Now it is time to stop talking about it and to focus our efforts on actually doing it. Take the advice he gives in the passage below.

Since we have these promises, dear friends, let us purify ourselves from everything that contaminates body and spirit, perfecting holiness out of reverence for God. (2 Corinthians 7:1, NIV)

Remember from the beginning, the Lord told us through the prophet Ezekiel that we begin by washing our body. As we do this, we understand that this is more than a simple washing. We are ceremonially obeying the Lord which opens the way for cleansing. Then we see that this cleansing is both for the body and the spirit. In the last chapter we looked at cleansing the outside and now we have learned about the process of being cleansed on the inside. Third, the Lord has a kingdom purpose in doing all these things for us. It is the Lord's plan and desire for us to live in holiness out of reverence for Him. Reflect on these things as you activate this promise in your life.

JACOB'S ACTIVATION PRAYER

Then Jacob said, "O God of my father Abraham and God of my father Isaac, the Lord who said to me, 'Return to your country and to your family, and I will deal well with you': I am not worthy of the least of all the mercies and of all the truth which You have shown Your servant; for I crossed over this Jordan with my staff, and now I have become two companies.

Deliver me, I pray, from the hand of my brother, from the hand of Esau; for I fear him, lest he come and attack me and the mother with the children. For You said, 'I will surely treat you well, and make your descendants as the sand of the sea, which cannot be numbered for multitude.'" (Genesis 32:9-12)

SELAH QUESTIONS

(Selah means to pause and meditate on these things.)

1. Name three of the generations in which the Lord released these promises.

_____

_____

_____

2. How can the Lord forget our transgressions?

_____

_____

_____

3. Explain the Lord's purpose in such a deep cleaning.

_____

_____

_____

4. Name some ways the Lord has done this in your life.

_____

_____

_____

5. What are the steps you should take in the process of activating your cleansing?

_____

_____

_____

6. Why is Yom Kippur so important for the Lord's people?

_____

_____

_____

7. How have you responded to the Lord's command to do His work?

_____

_____

_____

CHAPTER FOUR

Promise Three

I Will Give You a New Heart

I will give you a **new heart** and put a new spirit within you; *I will* take the heart of stone out of your flesh and give you a heart of flesh. (Ezekiel 36:26)

HEART CONDITION

In our basic nature, we all have a heart problem. When the natural heart becomes diseased, it loses its capacity to oxygenate vital parts of our bodies. If left untreated, the heart also progressively weakens and its capacity for providing life-giving oxygen and other necessary nutrients begins to slowly diminish. As this condition progresses the heart itself is continually reduced in strength. When all this is happening, we have learned that heart failure cannot be far behind. We know from all our medical research that a diseased heart is not able to receive and distribute what the body and the heart itself need to survive. Heart disease is one of the leading causes of death in adults.

The Lord uses this natural process to illustrate a spiritual principle. In the same way that natural hearts weaken and begin to fail, our spiritual hearts can do the same. As our spiritual heart weakens it becomes limited in its ability to feed the critical elements needed by our spiritual bodies. Many people are unaware of their slowly advancing heart problems. Instead of making changes to become more healthy, they continue to do the things which allow their heart to progressively get worse. Neglecting the needs of your spiritual heart can be as destructive as neglecting a failing natural heart. How can we heal our failing hearts? The Lord reveals His method of saving the spiritual heart in the passage below. Take the Lord's great advice in the last sentence of this revelation, "*Therefore turn and live!*"

> *Cast away from you all the transgressions which you have committed, and get yourselves a new heart and a new spirit. For why should you die, O house of Israel? For I have no pleasure in the death of one who dies, says the Lord God. "Therefore turn and live!*" (Ezekiel 18:31-32)

HOW IS YOUR HEART DOING TODAY?

Some people reading this question may immediately consider some disease or infirmity affecting their own natural heart. Congestive heart failure, cardiovascular disease, partially closed arteries, and other diseases may be a serious threat to your health and your life. Pause and consider this question: How is your heart doing today? One set of health-related statistics shows that one in every four deaths in the USA is related to heart disease. Some other statistics say that one in three people die from cardiovascular disease. These are alarming statistics and should cause us to take note and begin taking better care of our natural hearts. The question becomes: How do we do this? There are so many conflicting recommendations.

Many people turn exclusively to manmade treatments and medications to improve the condition of their hearts. Even with these medications, some people still experience a continuous decline in heart health. If you watch some of the advertisements for these medical treatments, it is very discouraging to hear all the possible side effects of these medications. It often sounds like the proposed remedy is worse than the disease. Many people with heart diseases fail to see that there is another treatment approach available to them. Yeshua ha Messiach is the great physician and He can give you a new heart. Please hear this, I am not saying that you should stop taking your medicine or quit seeing your doctor. I am saying that you should add the power and promise of the Lord to whatever else you are doing.

Knowing that you have a problem with your heart can be the source of fearful concern which may result in a feeling of profound heaviness in your mind and spirit. What can you do when you or someone you care for is faced with these challenges? Many people think of prayer as a last resort when it should be the first response on our part. If you have a heart problem, are you praying now? Has it helped? Perhaps this is a good time to claim this promise, activate its power, and receive the heart healing you need. Consider for a moment the words of Yeshua in Matthew 8:13, "*Then Jesus said to the centurion, 'Go your way; and as you have believed, so let it be done for you.' And his servant was healed that same hour.*" Unfortunately, many people have little or no faith in healing and are receiving exactly what they believe in this area. If you receive exactly what you believe, what will that look like? Now is a good time to remember that "*So then faith comes by hearing, and hearing by the word of God.*" Begin to read aloud over and over the healing promises in the Word of God.

Put your faith in Yeshua and begin to speak with increasingly greater faith what the Word of God says about healing. Remember the powerful healing promise in Isaiah 53:5, make the promise your own and say it aloud several times: "By His stripes, I am healed." Think about it and remember the power of reading the promises of God aloud over and over. Then move to Exodus 15:26b, "*I am the Lord who heals you.*" A woman with a chronic illness once declined when I offered to pray for her. She said that Jesus could not heal everyone and she claimed this outcome for her life and condition. This is not biblically correct and is false teaching. It is a manmade doctrine attempting to explain to people why they were not healed. Study the Word of God for yourself and think about the efficacy of Yeshua's ministry. *"And great multitudes followed Him, and He healed them all."* (Matthew 13:15) It does not say that He was only able to heal a few of them. After they received the Holy Spirit and His power, this was also said of the disciples of Yeshua. They too began to heal all who came to them. I long for us to move in that level of faith again. How about you?

WHAT KIND OF HEART?

When I began to work through the meaning of the Lord's promise in Ezekiel 36:26, I started by asking myself some questions. Perhaps you have also asked some of these same questions. First, I asked myself, "Is the Lord talking about our spirit which has often been called our heart in scripture?" At first, it appeared to me that the central focus was on healing a spiritual condition. Thinking this way I considered that the passage might be strictly pointing to the spiritual heart. It is simpler to think of the promise this way. I believe people tend to do this to avoid the challenge of asking the Lord to replace someone's, natural heart. Why? Because they have a lack of faith and do not expect it to happen.

As I read the promise over and over, my thoughts began to change, and I began to think that it might be something more. Repeatedly reading the promises aloud, I heard one phrase in the promise more and more clearly: *give you a heart of flesh."* The more I spoke this aloud, the more I focused on one important question: "Is it the blood pump in our bodies He is talking about in this passage"? What do you think? As you reflect on this, consider what it means when He clearly says "*I will give you a heart of flesh.*" I wanted to be certain that I was reading this promise correctly so I asked a few more questions. Was this originally said to make a comparison with a spiritual heart of stone or is it the real human heart?

This time of reflection slowed my progress in getting this book written, but I was certain that I needed to do a deeper study of this topic. I felt that I needed to decide based on my faith before I could continue writing. These questions are too important for us to make a snap decision that might not speak clearly to the Lord's intent for us. The obvious next step is to consider another question: "Is it both types of hearts"? You may want to do what I did and make a search on the phrase "your heart" in the Bible. I was thankful that I had an electronic Bible which made it much easier to do this type of search. So, I ask you: "What do you think?

I MADE A CHOICE

We cannot simply sit on the sidelines and remain noncommittal when we are faced with these questions. We must make a choice and move in the power of faith to fulfill these promises. I made a choice. I decided to believe that the Lord can restore both physical and spiritual hearts. I became most aware of this choice as I prayed for people with heart diseases.

After many of our ministry sessions, we have a time of prayer ministry for individual needs. I found that I was praying more and more for people with heart diseases. I was praying intently for them to receive a new heart believing the Lord was going to fulfill the promise.

The Lord answered these prayers for healing the heart many times and we saw people being healed and some who received a creative miracle when they received a new physical heart. When this happens it opens a time of extreme worship giving Him all the glory for who He is and for what He does. I turned the following verse into a prayer and a spiritual decree: "*But He was wounded for our transgressions, He was bruised for our iniquities; the chastisement for our peace was upon Him, and by His stripes, we are healed.*" (Isaiah 53:5) My prayer/decree is: "By His stripes, I am healed." I say it over and over until it manifests. Amen? As you seek healing, check your level of gratitude and praise. Who is receiving glory from your healing?

> *Bless the LORD, O my soul, and forget not all His benefits: Who forgives all your iniquities, Who heals all your diseases, Who redeems your life from destruction, Who crowns you with lovingkindness and tender mercies, Who satisfies your mouth with good things, so that your youth is renewed like the eagle's.* (Psalm 103:2-5)

As we have prayed over and over for people to be healed, I have noticed one problem. People testify that they have received a new heart, but then fill it back up with all kinds of negative things. Often when I see them again, they tell me that their physical heart is a problem again. People who receive a heart transplant in the natural can damage the new heart with old unhealthy habits. They need to change their lifestyle and diets to keep their healing. It is the same in the spiritual realm. If you want to keep your healing, you need to live in love and gratitude to the one who healed you. You need to follow His clear and specific directions for keeping your heart clean, healthy, and full of life. Consider this as you read what the Lord told Moses and the Children of Israel.

> *"If you diligently heed the voice of the Lord your God and do what is right in His sight, give ear to His commandments and keep all His statutes, I will put none of the diseases on you which I have brought on the Egyptians. For I am the Lord who heals you."* (Exodus 15:26)

WHY WE NEED GIFTS OF HEALINGS

> *But the manifestation of the Spirit is given to each one for the profit of all: for to one is given the word of wisdom through the Spirit, to another the word of knowledge through the same Spirit, to another faith by the same Spirit, to another **gifts of healings** by the same Spirit, to another the working of miracles, to another prophecy, to another discerning of spirits, to another different kinds of tongues, to another the*

interpretation of tongues. But one and the same
Spirit works all these things, distributing to each one
individually as He wills. (1 Corinthians 12:7-11)

From this passage, we learn that the Lord clearly understands that we need more than one type of healing. Some spirit-filled believers are given very special ministry gifts through the Holy Spirit to enable them to impart healing to other people. Some may be specially gifted to bring healing to the soul (mind and will) while others are gifted at physical or spiritual healings. Part of the Holy Spirit's plan is for people to specialize in specific areas of healing. This often happens after the healer has been healed of the same problem. It is possible that one person can have healing gifts for every area of need, but this is not often the case. It all depends on the calling and gifting of the Holy Spirit. It is all up to the will of God as ministered through the work of the Holy Spirit. Then people are blessed and gifted to work with Him in ministry.

As I shared above, we need to take some positive steps to keep our healing. Consider first the idea that when you receive a new heart you need to fill it with the good things of the Lord. People usually receive some clear directions about how to feed and care for a new heart. Medical science understands that you can destroy a new heart by feeding it foods that clog the arteries. If you gain more weight, you will put more strain on the heart which can cause it to go through premature disease. This is why I pray for people to be healed both physically and spiritually. One way I do this is by praying for people to get a new spiritual heart along with their new physical heart.

Here is something to think about. We do more harm to our hearts with our thoughts and words than by our physical actions. It is important to eat heart-healthy foods, but it is much more important to keep the heart free from spiritual defilement. Even the Lord's closest disciples can have hardened hearts at times. This is why Mark 6:52 reports: "*For they had not understood about the loaves, because their heart was hardened.*" To prevent the hardening of the arteries and hardening of the heart we need to follow Yeshua closely every day. If you want to remain well in spirit, soul and body take the good advice of the Great Physician, Yeshua ha Messiach.

> *So He said to them, "Are you thus without understanding also? Do you not perceive that whatever enters a man from outside cannot defile him, because it does not enter his heart but his stomach, and is eliminated, thus purifying all foods?" And He said, "What comes out of a man, that defiles a man. For from within, out of the heart of men, proceed evil thoughts, adulteries, fornications, murders, thefts, covetousness, wickedness, deceit, lewdness, an evil eye, blasphemy, pride, foolishness. All these evil things come from within and defile a man."* (Mark 7:18-23)

I have another spiritual reason for believing in the physical, spiritual, and emotional healing of the heart. I don't like to put limits on what the Lord can and will do. I reflect on what Yeshua said in Mark 9:23, "*Jesus said to him, 'If you can believe, all things are possible to him who believes.'*" The realm of the things which are possible for the Lord is greater than the human mind can fully comprehend. Here is a word of advice I apply in my walk with the Lord. Make it a habit to always ask Him to do above and beyond what you ask or think.

> *Now to Him who is able to do exceedingly abundantly above all that we ask or think, according to the power that works in us, to Him be glory in the church by Christ Jesus to all generations, forever and ever. Amen.* (Ephesians 3:20-21)

I encourage you once more to read aloud all the promises of God. Read them over and over until they become yours. Read them aloud until you can claim them by faith. Remember once again the teaching of the Apostle Paul: "*So then faith comes by hearing, and hearing by the word of God.*" (Romans 10:17) To hear the Word of God, someone needs to speak it. Let that someone be you. Remember the voice you trust most is your own. Think about it. The Lord has granted you the grace to read, receive, and activate His promises. Now is a good time to pause and read aloud this promise of the Lord once again to release more of its power into your heart!

> ***I will*** *give you a **new heart** and put a new spirit within you;* ***I will*** *take the heart of stone out of your flesh and give you a **heart of flesh**.* (Ezekiel 36:26)

ACTIVATION

I rise before dawn and cry for help; I have put my hope in your word. My eyes stay open through the watches of the night, that I may meditate on your promises. Hear my voice in accordance with your love; preserve my life, O Lord, according to your laws. Those who devise wicked schemes are near, but they are far from your law. Yet you are near, O Lord, and all your commands are true. Long ago I learned from your statutes that you established them to last forever. (Psalm 119:147-152)

David has always been the primary example for me of someone who knows how to activate the promises of the Lord. In the passage above he tells us about how he meditates on the Lord's promises during the watches of the night. He is confident that the Lord will keep His promises. As a result, David has put his trust in the Lord. After acknowledging the Lord and His amazing promises, David prays for very specific help in his times of need. The promises of the Lord are eternal and He will not go back on His word. Do you believe this? If not, pause and do some faith-building of your own. Ask the Holy Spirit to help you. Remember that faith is one of the spiritual gifts of the Holy Spirit.

Take the time to read aloud His promises once again. Then consider the fullness of this promise of the Lord for you. Think about what He is saying to you as He gives this promise anew through the prophet Ezekiel. This promise is like a complex network of a variety of things and you need to walk closely with Him to understand how to navigate your way through the process. In the short passage below, He has promised you not one but four powerful spiritual gifts. Think about what the Lord can and will do through your life if you let Him do all this for you. Then be filled with gratitude as you activate all these powerful promises in your life and ministry.

> *I will give you a new heart and put a __new spirit__ within you; I will take the heart of stone out of your flesh and give you a heart of flesh.* (Ezekiel 36:26)

1. HE WILL GIVE YOU A NEW HEART.

I see so many people who know that they need the Lord to give them a heart transplant. I see others who are completely unaware of their need for healing. Which type are you? It is not enough for the promises to be in the Word of God while we are completely unaware of them. It is not enough to know the promises are there but fail to receive and activate them. Don't make any of these common mistakes, but begin to believe for an uncommon miracle in your life. Claim it now and let the Lord activate it in your life.

2. HE WILL GIVE YOU A NEW SPIRIT.

We live in a world filled with people who are completely ignorant of the spiritual realm. They fail to receive because they do not know they have a need. Other people believe these biblical truths were once available, but that those times have long since passed. There are still others who believe the promises are for others but are not available to them. Don't make any of these mistakes. Believe the promises of God and open a way for Him to put all these things into you. All you need to do is believe what He says, receive the promises, and activate them in your life and ministry.

3. HE WILL TAKE THE HEART OF STONE OUT OF YOUR FLESH.

This sounds more like the physical heart but can also be your spiritual heart. Check out your own heart. Have you allowed your circumstances to harden your heart over time? This can happen so slowly that most people do not know it is happening. Ask the Lord to help you to become more fully aware of the condition of your heart. Remember that this is also one of the works of the Holy Spirit. Ask Him to reveal it to you. Then ask yourself if you want a heart transplant today? All you need to do is claim the promise right now. Ask the Holy Spirit to help you activate it. Then let your praise flow like a mighty river. Amen?

4. HE WILL GIVE YOU A HEART OF FLESH.

Expand your faith beyond what you have believed in the past. Always remember that the Lord is capable of creative miracles. He can give you replacement body parts. Nothing is beyond the Lord's ability to do what He says He will do. Hallelujah! I believe we all need this heart transplant and the Lord is so good to give it to those who ask. Amen? Remember what James taught us about praying without faith. As you reflect on the passage below, ask yourself if you have been double-minded. Have any of your prayers failed to produce results because you have not had faith in the Lord to keep His promises? If you find this to be true, pray for the Holy Spirit to help you overcome your weakness.

If any of you lacks wisdom, let him ask of God, who gives to all liberally and without reproach, and it will be given to him. But let him ask in faith, with no doubting, for he who doubts is like a wave of the sea driven and tossed by the wind. For let not that man suppose that he will receive anything from the Lord; he is a double-minded man, unstable in all his ways. (James 1:5-8)

SEVEN POWERFUL PRAISES

Praise is one of the powerful tools the Lord has given to us as a way of activating His promises in our lives. To the immature, it appears that we are giving the Lord something of value to Him. This may be our motive in our praise, but it is not how things work in the spiritual realm. Praise is not truly a gift to the Lord because He has more than earned all we can ever give. Think about this. It is an honor to be allowed to praise Him. Consider this as you read the passage below:

Blessed be the God and Father of our Lord Jesus Christ, who has blessed us with every spiritual blessing in the heavenly places in Christ, just as He chose us in Him before the foundation of the world, that we should be holy and without blame before Him in love, having predestined us to adoption as sons by Jesus Christ to Himself, according to the good pleasure of His will, to the praise of the glory of His grace, by which He made us accepted in the Beloved. (Ephesians 1:3-6)

The mature believer understands that our praise of the Lord blesses us. As we praise Him we open channels of grace and the flow of gifts from the Lord. Paul referred to this as he wrote of all the things the Lord has already done for us. The things He has already done are enough to motivate us to give him constant praise and glory for eternity. The Lord has *"blessed us with every spiritual blessing in the heavenly places in Christ."* What more can He do when He has already given us everything available in the spiritual realm. Praise the Lord now to open the way for Him to release all these things to you. The Lord has provided a wonderful summary for you in the passage below. Don't just read it. Praise your way through it and see what the Lord will do.

Halleluyah!

1. Praise Adonai from the heavens!

2. Praise him in the heights!

3. Praise him, all His angels!

4. Praise him, all His armies!

5. Praise him, sun and moon!

6. Praise him, all shining stars!

7. Praise him, highest heaven, and waters above the heavens!

Let them praise the name of Adonai; for he commanded and they were created. He also established them forever and ever; he has given a law to which they must conform. (Psalm 148:1-6, CJB)

AMAZING RESULTS OF PRAISE

I WILL PUT MY SPIRIT INSIDE YOU

The Lord has promised over and over that He is willing to put His Spirit in us. As you study the Word of God, you hear Him declare it afresh for every generation. Do you think He has suddenly stopped short of making the promises available for our generation? This is not how the Lord operates. He is by nature a giver, and His nature and His spiritual attributes are for all believers for all eternity. The promises are as real and as powerful today as when they were first spoken. Believe it so that you can receive all He has prepared for you. Don't live in spiritual poverty, when the wealth of Heaven is available for you. Amen?

*Yet hear me now, O Jacob My servant, and Israel whom I have chosen. Thus says the Lord who made you and formed you from the womb, who will help you: 'Fear not, O Jacob My servant; and you, Jeshurun, whom I have chosen. For **I will** pour water on him who is thirsty, and floods on the dry ground; **I will pour My Spirit** on your descendants, and My blessing on your offspring; they will spring up among the grass like willows by the watercourses.' One will say, 'I am the Lord's'; another will call himself by the name of Jacob; another will write with his hand, 'The Lord's', and name himself by the name of Israel.* (Isaiah 44:1-5)

PRAYER FOR CLEANSING THE HEART

Purge me with hyssop, and I shall be clean; wash me, and I shall be whiter than snow. Make me hear joy and gladness, that the bones You have broken may rejoice. Hide Your face from my sins, and blot out all my iniquities. Create in me a clean heart, O God, and renew a steadfast spirit within me. Do not cast me away from Your presence, and do not take Your Holy Spirit from me. Restore to me the joy of Your salvation, and uphold me by Your generous Spirit. Then I will teach transgressors Your ways, and sinners shall be converted to You. (Psalm 51:7-13)

SELAH QUESTIONS

(Selah means to pause and meditate on these things.)

1. When the Lord speaks of giving us a new heart, do you think He is pointing to a real heart in the physical or a spiritual heart? Explain why you believe this.

_____

_____

_____

2. Does the Lord give some people a new physical heart? Can you give an example?

_____

_____

_____

3. Have you experienced His promise of a new heart in your own life? In what way?

_____

_____

_____

4. Can you name more than one type of heart healing?

_____

_____

_____

5. What can Praise release in your life?

_____

_____

_____

6. How can you activate this promise in your own life?

_____

_____

_____

CHAPTER FIVE

Promise Four

I Will Put My Spirit Inside You

*"**I will put My Spirit inside you** and cause you to live by My laws, respect my rulings and obey them. You will live in the land I gave to your ancestors. You will be my people, and I will be your God."* (Ezekiel 36:27-28, CJB)

The Lord promises to give an amazing gift to those who have been through His cleansing process. What is this gift? Think about it. He will put His Spirit inside those He has chosen and cleansed. This is why the promises are given in this order. The Spirit of the Lord can only reside in us after the temple (which is now in our hearts) has been cleansed and purified. Only clean and purified hearts can house His Holy Spirit. We see in this move of the Lord which was revealed to us through Ezekiel, that there is a progressive process of the Lord at work in these promises. Step by step He makes His promises effective in the lives of those who choose to follow Him. In past eras, this gift was only given to a few very special people who had been called as prophets or national leaders. It is now available to all believers.

Remember how Peter made this announcement on the day of Shavuot (Pentecost). Peter, standing up with the eleven, raised his voice and said to them,

> "*Men of Judea and all who dwell in Jerusalem, let this be known to you, and heed my words.*
>
> *For these are not drunk, as you suppose, since it is only the third hour of the day.*
>
> *But this is what was spoken by the prophet Joel:* 'And it shall come to pass in the last days, says God, that **I will pour out of My Spirit on all flesh**; your sons and your daughters shall prophesy, your young men shall see visions, your old men shall dream dreams. And on My menservants and on My maidservants **I will pour out My Spirit** in those days; and they shall prophesy. (Acts 2:14-18)

Remember that when the Lord says something twice it is fixed and certain. He gave the promise of putting His Spirit in us over and over in different generations. Think about it. This promise was given through the prophet Ezekiel on two different occasions (Ezekiel 36:27 and Ezekiel 37:14). It was then prophesied in greater detail through the Prophet Joel (Joel

2:28-29). Centuries later more was revealed as Peter explained that this promise had been fulfilled on the Day of Pentecost.

The Lord gave three conditions that must be met for people to receive this awesome gift. First, people need to make a lifestyle change which includes a decision to walk in His laws. More specifically this means to follow His statutes and decrees. For those who love and trust the Lord, this will not be drudgery or some kind of hardship. "*The statutes of the Lord are right, rejoicing the heart; the commandment of the Lord is pure, enlightening the eyes*; (Psalm 19:8)" The second condition for people who want to be filled with His Spirit, is to respect His rulings. I believe that a spirit of rebellion is born into each one of us. This is a tendency which we must constantly resist and daily strengthen and increase our choice to respect whatever the Lord requests of us in our lives and ministries. This leads us to the third condition for being filled with His Spirit. You must be willing to obey. This has been the experience of many people during seasons of revival. People who have experienced powerful moves of revival learned that they must obey the Lord quickly and explicitly to open and keep open the way for the Holy Spirit to continue to manifest. These revivalists have learned the great price paid by those who grieve the Holy Spirit.

THE LORD GIVES MORE AND MORE

The Lord has been mindful of us; He will bless us; He will bless the house of Israel; He will bless the house of Aaron. He will bless those who fear the Lord, both small and great. May the Lord give you increase more and more, you and your children. May you be blessed by the Lord, Who made heaven and earth. (Psalm 115:12-15)

Have you noticed that as you receive and activate one of the Lord's promises, He immediately releases more? The passage of scripture above is a personal favorite for me. In our meetings in South Korea, I have used this passage over and over. Because of my habit of always seeking more from the Lord, some of the people began to call me "Pastor More." Then as now, I invite people to join the "More" family. How about you? Are you ready to receive more? I especially like the idea that the Lord gives "*increase more and more.*" I also love the promise that the Lord's gift of increase will also be given to my children. The Lord is so awesome.

Look again at the promise we are receiving in this chapter. He promises to give us a new spirit and then adds to it by promising to give us His Spirit. The Holy Spirit is given to live inside us. How do you answer the question Paul asks in 1 Corinthians 3:16? "*Do you not know that you are the temple of God and that the Spirit of God dwells in you?*" If the Spirit of God is not living in you, it is time for you to claim the promise and activate it in your life, family, and ministry. Remember the words of Yeshua given in Luke 11:13, "*If you then, being evil, know how to give good gifts to your children, how much more will your heavenly Father give the Holy Spirit to those who ask Him!*" Yeshua reaffirms the Lord's promise and gives the guarantee that He will do it. Amen?

THIS SOUNDS LIKE THE PROMISED BAPTISM OF THE HOLY SPIRIT.

In Matthew 3:11, John the Baptizer gives a powerful prophetic word for us: "*I indeed baptize you with water unto repentance, but He who is coming after me is mightier than I, whose sandals I am not worthy to carry. He will baptize you with the Holy Spirit and fire.*" This promise came in two stages. The first stage of the impartation of the promise was fulfilled by Yeshua just before His ascension. It is recorded in John 20:22, "*And when He had said this, He breathed on them, and said to them, "Receive the Holy Spirit.* Near the time of His crucifixion, Yeshua told His disciples that they had a learning blockage. Not a natural blockage, but a spiritual blockage. He promised that this blockage would be removed after His death when the Spirit of truth was going to be given to them.

> *I still have many things to say to you, but you cannot bear them now. However, when He, the Spirit of truth, has come, He will guide you into all truth; for He will not speak on His own authority, but whatever He hears He will speak; and He will tell you things to come.* (John 16:12-13)

Some of the parts of Yeshua's kingdom teaching needed to wait until His disciples were enabled to receive them. So Yeshua made a promise that He would send the Holy Spirit in the form of the Spirit of truth to help them learn. In the natural, you cannot understand the teachings about the Kingdom of God, because they are spiritually discerned. In John 14:16-17, the Lord gave them a clear picture of this when He said, "*And I will pray the Father, and He will give you another Helper, that He may abide with you forever—the Spirit of truth, whom the world cannot receive, because it neither sees Him nor knows Him; but you know Him, for He dwells with you and will be in you.*" Yeshua fulfilled this promise when He breathed the Spirit into them. After this, we see that Yeshua taught them more about the Kingdom of God during the forty days He spent with them after the resurrection. This all happened just as Yeshua had taught and promised. The Holy Spirit filled them and quicken their spirits to hear and learn these greater kingdom principles and truths. Remember those words at the end of the passage above: "*He dwells with you and will be in you.*" The great promise given through the prophet Ezekiel was now fulfilled in the ministry of Yeshua.

The second phase of the promise given through John the Baptizer came on Shavuot. The baptism of fire was first given in the Upper Room as the disciples gathered in obedience to Yeshua. They didn't gather to do things and say prayers that would qualify them for the baptism of fire. We can never do enough good to qualify ourselves for this amazing gift. It is a promise of God. In the passage below you will see that Yeshua named it "the Promise of the Father."

We must always remember that we are qualified because of what Yeshua did. The promise of the Father is an impartation of the fire of God. See Acts 2:3-4, "*Then there appeared to them divided tongues, as of fire, and one sat upon each of them. And they were all filled with the Holy Spirit and began to speak with other tongues, as the Spirit gave them utterance.*" This was and is the great fulfillment of this amazing promise given by Father God. Think about what it means for you as you study the passage below.

> And being assembled together with them, He commanded them not to depart from Jerusalem, but to wait for the Promise of the Father, "which," He said, "you have heard from Me; for John truly baptized with water, but **you shall be baptized with the Holy Spirit** not many days from now." Therefore, when they had come together, they asked Him, saying, "Lord, will You at this time restore the kingdom to Israel?" And He said to them, "It is not for you to know times or seasons which the Father has put in His own authority. But **you shall receive power when the Holy Spirit has come upon you;** and you shall be witnesses to Me in Jerusalem, and in all Judea and Samaria, and to the end of the earth." (Acts 1:4-8)

This is all very good news if you can believe it and receive it. Many believers today are not certain if this is still possible. Some claim it ended on that first Shavuot. I don't believe this for two powerful reasons. First, it is based on clear scriptural principles. It is also my testimony from my personal experience of this baptism of fire. It is clear in the New Testament that second and third-generation believers received this gift of the Holy Spirit. Consider Paul's ministry in Corinth. "*And when Paul had laid hands on them, the Holy Spirit came upon them, and they spoke with tongues and prophesied.*" (Acts 19:6) See also Acts 8:17, "*Then they laid hands on them, and they received the Holy Spirit.*"

The Lord has not withdrawn His promise or withheld any of the good things of Heaven from His children. The things the Lord has given in the past, He still gives today. Remember the powerful message given in Hebrews 13:8, "*Jesus Christ is the same yesterday, today, and forever.*" Also, think about Paul's testimony in Ephesians 1:3, "*Blessed be the God and Father of our Lord Jesus Christ, who has blessed us with every spiritual blessing in the heavenly places in Christ,*" If you haven't received the fulfillment of this promise yet, perhaps it is time for you to accept this powerful promise and activate it by faith in your life. Look again at the promise given through Ezekiel as you receive and activate this amazing and powerful promise:

> "*I will put My Spirit inside you* *and cause you to live by My laws, respect my rulings and obey them. You will live in the land I gave to your ancestors. You will be my people, and I will be your God.*" (Ezekiel 36:27-28, CJB)

PROMISES ARE INTERCONNECTED

As I was writing this portion of the book the Lord suddenly gave me another revelation. The Lord reminded me of the promises given to Moses in the wilderness about His plan to redeem His people, the children of Israel. For more details see book No. 1 in this series called, *"Redemption"*. I began to see more clearly that all the Lord's promises given through the centuries are all tied together. Theologians often speak of "salvation history" as we begin to see that the Lord is working a grand process to return us to the state of grace which existed in the Garden of Eden before the fall of man. This is a powerful reminder that this has been the Lord's plan from the beginning. He has been clear about it, but many of us have not recognized the movement in our generations. It is time to wake up and let the Spirit of truth in us guide us into a more complete understanding of what the Lord has planned and to see how He is working that plan for us in our generation. Amen?

Each generation of human beings has been called back to the basics of their relationship with Father God. From beginning to end we see the Word of God being encountered over and again for each generation. Now, in our generation, the Lord is releasing the promises once again. As we can see clearly from His Word, He is preparing a bride to be clean and holy for the coming time of our ultimate reunion with Him. How will this generation respond to this move of God which is essentially like every previous move? Think about it. The Lord is going to do this once more in our generation. Are you prepared to receive it and activate all His promises? What He did for Moses and the people, He did again in Ezekiel's generation. The Lord plans to continue to do it for you and me. Amen?

You will live in the land I gave to your ancestors. You will be my people, and I will be your God." (Ezekiel 36:28, CJB)

THE LORD MOVED IN ISAIAH'S GENERATION.

Yet hear me now, O Jacob My servant, and Israel whom I have chosen. Thus says the Lord who made you and formed you from the womb, who will help you: 'Fear not, O Jacob My servant; and you, Jeshurun, whom I have chosen. **For I will pour water on him** *who is thirsty, and floods on the dry ground;* **I will pour My Spirit** *on your descendants, and My blessing on your offspring; they will spring up among the grass like willows by the watercourses.' One will say, 'I am the Lord's'; another will call himself by the name of Jacob; another will write with his hand, 'The Lord's', and name himself by the name of Israel.* (Isaiah 44:1-5)

The passage above became the theme of the Hebrides Revival. The Hebrides is a chain of Islands just off the coast of Scotland which had a mighty revival in the middle of the last century. The intercessors understood the generational connection in

God's promises and rightly believed they could place a claim on the Lord's promises and receive what He had released to others in the past. The Lord is now calling for us to be ready for His revival in our time. Are you ready? What are you doing to prepare? Like the great revivals of the past, we need to place a claim on the promises of God. We need to receive them by faith and activate them to release their power in another season with a different group of people. Will you be one of them?

WHAT HE DID IN PAST GENERATIONS HE PROMISES TO DO FOR US RIGHT NOW

> *Jesus answered and said to him, "If anyone loves Me, he will keep My word; and My Father will love him, and We will come to him and make Our home with him. He who does not love Me does not keep My words; and the word which you hear is not Mine but the Father's who sent Me.* (John 14:23-24)

Yeshua didn't bring an end to the need for us to be obedient to the Word of God in the Torah and the rest of the Old Testament. With each new generation, He required greater levels of obedience. Look again at the words of Yeshua in Matthew 5:21-34. Over and over He speaks of the requirements of the law and then says, "But I say unto you…" Then He followed that with a stricter interpretation of the Lord's will. One of the most difficult lessons for many to accept is

found in Matthew 5:43-45a, *"You have heard that it was said,
'You shall love your neighbor and hate your enemy.' But I say
to you, love your enemies, bless those who curse you, do good
to those who hate you, and pray for those who spitefully use
you and persecute you, that you may be sons of your Father
in heaven;"*

Yeshua breathed new life into the ancient requirements of
the Torah. In His Kingdom teaching, Yeshua connected
the requirements of the Father's teachings, guidelines, and
principles given to Moses centuries before with a process of
building and maintaining relationships. He did this by linking
the Torah principles with a renewed relationship with Father
God. What Yeshua taught almost sounded too good to be
true for those who first heard it, but all of it was exactly what
the Father had intended all along. As it turns out, the basic
principles were all designed to help us learn to love the Father
and all His children. This had been in the Torah all along, but
people had gotten too focused on the rules and regulations.
They lost sight of the primary principle

> *For if you love those who love you, what reward have
> you? Do not even the tax collectors do the same?
> And if you greet your brethren only, what do you do
> more than others? Do not even the tax collectors do
> so? Therefore you shall be perfect, just as your Father
> in heaven is perfect.* (Matthew 5:46-48)

As I studied this teaching, I once again started to ask some
questions. First: How can we be made perfect? Is it possible

for human beings to be perfect as the Father is perfect? Remember what Yeshua prayed in John 17:22-23, *"And the glory which You gave Me I have given them, that they may be one just as We are one: I in them, and You in Me; that they may be made perfect in one, and that the world may know that You have sent Me, and have loved them as You have loved Me."* It is clear in both the New and Old Testaments that our perfection is God's plan.

But how can we ever reach this status with the Lord? Here is the good news of the Gospel of Yeshua ha Messiach. This does not happen through our good works but by the righteous works of Yeshua ha Messiach. Many believers have told me they cannot accept this idea. They don't think it is true. But it is true, and it is promised to you. It is a promise. He will put His Spirit in you and seal these promises for you. Remember what Paul taught in Ephesians 1:13-14, *"In Him you also trusted, after you heard the word of truth, the gospel of your salvation; in whom also, having believed, you were sealed with the Holy Spirit of promise, who is the guarantee of our inheritance until the redemption of the purchased possession, to the praise of His glory."* Consider again this amazing promise as you study the section below.

I WILL PUT MY SPIRIT IN YOU

If you love Me, keep My commandments. And I will pray the Father, and He will give you another Helper, that He may abide with you forever—the Spirit of truth, whom the world cannot receive, because it neither sees Him nor knows Him; but you know Him, for He dwells with you and will be in you. I will not leave you orphans; I will come to you. (John 14:15-18)

This was one of Yeshua's most often taught subjects. Notice the powerful "I will" statements in the passage above. Also notice that Yeshua reaffirms that you can count on the promises of the Father. The Lord releases so much assurance for you and me in this teaching. I recommend that you make a careful search for and study of all of Yeshua's "I will" promises. Read them aloud over and over. Then receive them by faith and activate them in your life and ministry. For now, focus on the promises of Yeshua in the above passage. He says that He will pray for you. That is so awesome. Further, He promises to pray for the Father to give you another "Helper' who will abide with you forever. That is also an amazing and wonderful promise to me. How about you? He will put His Spirit in you.

You can trust Him. He will do what He promises. Remember that generation after generation has testified that He has kept all His promises. Not even one of them has failed for those who are united with Him in the Holy Spirit. Next claim another "I will" promise of Yeshua: "*I will not leave you orphans;*" You will never be abandoned by the Lord. If you don't feel close to Him right now, it is not because He has left you. You may need to look at your behavior and attitudes to discover why you don't feel close to the Lord. Trust Him! He keeps His promises. Believe and receive all He has released to you in His Word.

Or do you think that the Scripture says in vain, "The Spirit who dwells in us yearns jealously"? But He gives more grace. Therefore He says: "God resists the proud, but gives grace to the humble." (James 4:5-6)

The third promise of Yeshua given in John 14:18 is: "*I will come to you.*" For some people, this is a scary thought because they know that they are not ready for Him to appear. These people know that they have failed the obedience test over and over. Unfortunately, some of these people ignore this promise, hoping it will not happen in their lifetime. The real act of wisdom on our part is to repent and return so that we can accept the promise and be enabled by His grace to be acceptable to Him. I love the way James says it: "*The Spirit who dwells in us yearns jealously"? But He gives more grace.* (James 4:5b-6a) Remember that all of this happens through the grace and mercy of the Lord. He gives grace to the humble and He resists the proud. Which are you?

IT IS IMPORTANT TO REMEMBER: THIS PROMISE COMES WITH REQUIREMENTS.

Jesus answered and said to him, "If anyone loves Me, he will keep My word; and My Father will love him, and We will come to him and make Our home with him. He who does not love Me does not keep My words; and the word which you hear is not Mine but the Father's who sent Me. (John 14:23-24)

This promise flows as long as obedience flows. Remember that Yeshua never removed or replaced this requirement. The fact is that He made it clearer than the prophets of old. If you love Him, you will most certainly obey Him. If you do not obey, it means that you do not truly love Him. Does this seem too difficult to understand? Remember the Good News: Even this requirement for obedience is a work of the Lord. He said He would cause us to walk in His laws. He will do this by teaching us to respect His judgments and rulings and then being careful to obey them. Consider this as you study the three passages below.

> *Hold fast the pattern of sound words which you have heard from me, in faith and love which are in Christ Jesus. That good thing which was committed to you, keep by the Holy Spirit who dwells in us.* (2 Timothy 1:13-14)

In this passage, the Apostle Paul is mentoring his young assistant. He desires to give him what he needs to be a successful disciple of Yeshua ha Messiach. You can allow this to be one of your mentoring sessions from Paul. On social media, I am hearing the strangest forms of how people are attempting to teach the gospel. Many of them are unaware of or have abandoned the sound words of scripture. Paul advises us to hold fast to sound words along with the pattern in which they are given. The good news is that the Holy Spirit has been given to assist us in doing these things. So the primary advice is to hold fast to the gift of God in you: the Holy Spirit. Amen?

Do you not know that you are the temple of God and that the Spirit of God dwells in you? If anyone defiles the temple of God, God will destroy him. For the temple of God is holy, which temple you are. (1 Corinthians 3:16-17)

The Lord replaced the Temple in Jerusalem after it was destroyed. He multiplied the outreach of the Temple through the disciples of Yeshua. Now there are millions of temples residing in His true followers. Then the Apostle warns us that there are some rules for keeping the Temple of God undefiled. When the Father, the Son, and the Holy Spirit come to reside in you, you have a responsibility to keep His house clean and holy so He can continue to reside there. How clean is your temple? Perhaps it is time to do some house cleaning of your own. I strongly advise you not to grieve the Holy Spirit. What can you do without Him working in your life and ministry?

But you are not in the flesh but in the Spirit, if indeed the Spirit of God dwells in you. Now if anyone does not have the Spirit of Christ, he is not His. And if Christ is in you, the body is dead because of sin, but the Spirit is life because of righteousness. But if the Spirit of Him who raised Jesus from the dead dwells in you, He who raised Christ from the dead will also give life to your mortal bodies through His Spirit who dwells in you. (Romans 8:9-11)

I have found that most people like to hear that they are spiritual beings temporarily living in a house of flesh. This is our hope for eternity and it can give you great assurance when the way becomes difficult. I like to hear that the one who raised Yeshua from the dead is residing in me in power to give life to my mortal body. How about you? We should think more about our spiritual being than our physical being. The tent in which we reside for now will soon pass away, but the Spirit of God in us makes us into eternal beings. Thanks be to Father God! Amen. Take a few moments to receive and activate this promise again in your life. Consider again the promise of the Lord: "I will put my Spirit inside you."

ACTIVATION

Since we have these promises, dear friends, let us purify ourselves from everything that contaminates body and spirit, perfecting holiness out of reverence for God. (2 Corinthians 7:1, NIV)

Paul had some advice for his readers about how to activate the Lord's promises in their lives. First, it is critically important to know and understand the promises. You cannot activate something you don't know you have. Next, Paul advises us to purify ourselves, and this is exactly what we have been studying in this chapter. Now it is time to do it. This cleansing is both for the body and the spirit. In the last chapter we looked at cleansing the outside and now we have learned about the process of being cleansed on the inside. Third, there is a kingdom purpose of the Lord activated when we do these things. It is the Lord's plan and desire for us to live in holiness out of reverence for the Father. Reflect on these things as you activate this promise in your life.

SELAH QUESTIONS

(Selah means to pause and meditate on these things.)

1. How has a spirit of rebellion limited people's ability to receive His promise?

_____

_____

_____

2. How can you know that the promises are for each generation?

_____

_____

_____

3. What did Yeshua teach about receiving the Holy Spirit?

_____

_____

_____

4. If you have received this gift, how has it impacted your life?

_____

_____

_____

5. What are the requirements to receive and retain the promises of the Holy Spirit?

_____

_____

_____

6. Have you activated this gift in your own life and ministry?

_____

_____

_____

7. If not, what steps do you need to take to activate it right now?

_____

_____

_____

CHAPTER SIX

Promise Five

I Will Save You From Uncleanliness

I will deliver you from all your uncleannesses. (Ezekiel 36:29a)

As I reached this point in the writing of this book, it occurred to me that it would be a good idea to read and review the previous promises to keep them fresh in our minds. I believe that it is important to keep all the promises we looked at previously in mind as we approach each new one. I also believe we release more power and put more faith into each of the promises every time we read them aloud. I remind you once again of the powerful word in Romans 10:17, "*So then faith comes by hearing, and hearing by the word of God.*" By doing this, you truly make the promises your own. Do you agree? I hope you do.

So I invite you to read, receive, and activate the Lord's promises once again. Okay? Repetition is one powerful way to learn a topic. Think about the teaching of the Apostle in 2 Peter 1:12, *"So I will always remind you of these things, even though you know them and are firmly established in the truth you now have."* Even though you know certain kingdom principles, you can grow stronger by hearing them again. Repetition is a powerful tool for use in the learning process. Do not despise it. With this in mind, let us review the promises of the Lord to anchor them in our souls. These promises are found in Ezekiel 36:25-28.

1. *Then I will sprinkle clean water on you, and you shall be clean;* (Ezekiel 36:25a, CJB)

> Read it aloud several times to anchor it in your spirit. When it is anchored, take an action step to receive it and activate it. Remain aware that this is a work of the Lord and not of your own doing. He makes all these things available to you and then adds His power to accomplish these promises in your life. Each time you activate a promise, remember to respond with praise and thanksgiving as you give all the credit to the Lord. I recommend that you begin to give glory to the Lord even before the promises manifest. This is a clear demonstration of your faith which also opens the way in your heart for the Lord to do this awesome work.

2. *I will cleanse you from all your filthiness and from all your idols.* (Ezekiel 36:25b, CJB)

Some people struggle with the idea of accepting and acknowledging their need for this cleansing. In other words, they are not spiritually aware of their need and fail to see why they should take this step. Also, many people have difficulty with the idea that they have idols in their hearts. As I considered this idea, I was reminded by the Holy Spirit of what the Lord said in Ezekiel 14:2-3, "*Then the word of the Lord came to me: 'Son of man, these men have set up idols in their hearts and put wicked stumbling blocks before their faces. Should I let them inquire of me at all?'*" The tragedy of the idols in our hearts is that they blind our eyes to the truth and leave us unaware of their presence. When this happens, we fail to take the steps which are necessary to remove them. Once again, ask the Spirit of Truth to reveal all that you need to know so that you can deal with any troubling issues in your life and walk with the Lord.

3. *I will give you a new heart and put a new spirit within you; I will take the heart of stone out of your flesh and give you a heart of flesh.* (Ezekiel 36:26)

Remember that the Lord is speaking of both the physical and spiritual heart. This is why we need "gifts of healings" from the Holy Spirit. People need healing and cleansing in their spirits, souls, and bodies. To be fully set free spiritually, you need for all these areas to be cleansed and healed. This is why the Lord takes this powerful step of putting a new heart in us as He removes the heart of stone. Consider all the ways the Lord is healing and cleansing you. When you accept these gifts of God, it should motivate you to greater and greater levels of praise and thanksgiving.

4. *I will put My Spirit within you and cause you to walk in My statutes, and you will keep My judgments and do them.* (Ezekiel 36:27)

We need to do some house cleaning if we are going to be able to prepare the way for the Lord to put His Spirit in us. When the Temple in our heart is cleansed and occupied by the Holy Spirit, some additional things need to be changed. We need to dedicate ourselves once again to become consistently obedient to the Lord. We should have a growing love and appreciation for His statutes and judgments. We should be motivated to be obedient to all that the Lord desires of us. At this point, something shifts in our spiritual experience. We begin to receive what the Lord has always promised for His people. Remember the words of the Psalmist, "*Oh, how I love Your law! It is my meditation all the day. You, through Your commandments, make me wiser than my enemies;*" (Psalm 119:97) In this passage, the psalmist lists several wonderful benefits coming to Him from the love of the Lord's Torah. Study the list below and allow the Lord to activate all these benefits in your life and work.

a. *I have more understanding than all my teachers, For Your testimonies are my meditation.* (v. 99)
b. *I understand more than the ancients, because I keep Your precepts.* (v. 100)

c. *I have restrained my feet from every evil way, that I may keep Your word.* (v. 101)

d. *How sweet are Your words to my taste, sweeter than honey to my mouth!* (v. 103)

e. *Through Your precepts I get understanding; therefore I hate every false way.* (v. 104)

When we love and obey the Lord and follow His teachings, all these powerful benefits become available to us. The really good news is that He continues to give more and more through His grace. The Lord accepts us as His family and invites us to dwell in the land of promise and live in His Shalom glory. I love the way the Lord reaches out to us and invites us to live in the fullness He has planned from the beginning. Think about how awesome the offer is in the following passage of scripture.

Then you shall dwell in the land that I gave to your fathers; you shall be My people, and I will be your God. (Ezekiel 36:28)

NOW WE MOVE INTO PROMISE FIVE.

I will deliver you from all your uncleannesses. (Ezekiel 36:29a)

I found the word "*uncleannesses*" very interesting. My computer does not accept it as being spelled correctly. As I reflected on this, I was reminded that the dictionary is a manmade product. Only the words available in the natural reasoning of the author are accepted as accurate. I began to meditate on what the word truly means in the spiritual realm. Then I saw clearly that the Lord plans to deliver us on several different levels. Each level has a different set of tools and methods of deliverance. Only the tools provided by the Lord will work in each of these areas. It became obvious to me that the Lord wants to deliver us in spirit, soul, and body. I am ready for it. How about you?

Notice that promise number five is very much like the promises of Redemption given to the Children of Israel in Egypt. We see the Lord taking another generation from under the burdens placed on them by an enemy and rescuing them to enter into His promised place of blessing, favor, and rest. At the same time that people are receiving His deliverance, they are beginning to enjoy a new and deeper relationship with Him. The good news is that Father God is still in the redemption business. He still saves to the utmost all those who believe in Him. He still offers this promise to His people today. It is still His plan to deliver each of us. It is His promise and He always keeps His promises. Think about it personally. This awesome promise is being released once more and it is for you and me! Amen?

Have you already discovered that the Lord repeats all of these extremely important prophetic promises to each generation? Now it is our turn and He desires to give us what He has given throughout history. It has not diminished over time. His strength has not weakened in the slightest degree. To make that very clear, He has already spoken these things through Moses, Isaiah, and Ezekiel. Now He releases them once again for you. Think about this as you read more of His promises. Also, think about the prophetic and spiritual significance when the Lord says something twice. This means it is fixed and certain. It also means that it will soon manifest. It is available in every generation and every circumstance. This is not an old and forgotten promise. It is new every day as His people continue to receive it. Think about how awesome it is that His promises have now be made available for you and me.

> *Then I will give them one heart, and I will put a new spirit within them, and take the stony heart out of their flesh, and give them a heart of flesh, that they may walk in My statutes and keep My judgments and do them; and they shall be My people, and I will be their God.* (Ezekiel 11:19-20)

It is no accident that the Lord speaks these promises over and over from generation to generation. It is Father God's character and His will to bless all His children. Once again we see that to receive it, activate it, and walk in it, we must be willing to obey His statutes and follow His judgments. It is not enough to merely know them. We must also do them. We have a good example in the Book of Job. Job made a covenant with his eyes not to look on things that might tempt him. He made a plan and followed it to keep his relationship with the Lord clean and strong. His plan worked. We know this because the Lord calls Job a righteous man.

I made a covenant with my eyes not to look lustfully at a girl. For what is man's lot from God above, his heritage from the Almighty on high? Is it not ruin for the wicked, disaster for those who do wrong? Does he not see my ways and count my every step? (Job 31:1-4, NIV)

TYPES OF UNCLEANNESS

In the previous chapter, we saw that there are many types of illnesses and spiritual conditions which require a variety of different healing methods and gifts. As I mentioned above, the same is true for the conditions of spiritual uncleanness. This condition may exist in one or all of the three parts which make up who we are. In other words, we may have uncleanness in our spirits, souls, and/or bodies. This promise makes it clear that the Lord is going to use a variety of spiritual methods to bring about our cleansing and deliverance. In the section below meditate on the various ways the Lord deals with the conditions of uncleanness. To better understand this, I will break it down into the areas of spirit, soul, and body.

1. SPIRITUAL

This I say, therefore, and testify in the Lord, that you should no longer walk as the rest of the Gentiles walk, in the futility of their mind, having their understanding darkened, being alienated from the life of God, because of the ignorance that is in them, because of the blindness of their heart; who, being past feeling, have given themselves over to lewdness, to work all uncleanness with greediness. (Ephesians 4:17-19)

This is a powerful message about the spiritually destructive things which many people do to themselves. Their actions will eventually bring peril to their own lives and ministries. People are responsible and will be held accountable for their spiritual uncleanness. Note that these people bring uncleanness upon themselves. This should never be the spiritual condition of those who believe in Yeshua. Our goal is to live our lives in ways that please and honor Him. He promises to help us if we are willing to follow His plan and practices.

As we look deeper into Paul's teaching, we see that people are led into these conditions because of the futility of their thinking and the darkness of their understanding. Eventually, this will result in the spiritual condition of being alienated from the life of God. Don't live any longer in ignorance and spiritual blindness. This type of lifestyle results in a profound uncleanness in spirit as well as soul and body. It can also point to a form of demonic oppression as referenced in the passage below from the Revelation of John.

And I saw three unclean spirits like frogs coming out of the mouth of the dragon, out of the mouth of the beast, and out of the mouth of the false prophet. (Revelation 16:13)

The enemy uses demonic influences to bring uncleanness upon the Lord's people. Balaam could not curse the people who had been blessed by the Lord. However, his desire for the reward offered by the enemy of the people led him to come up with a plan to tempt the people into becoming unclean knowing that they would lose their protective covering from the Lord. Tragically the plan worked and the people suffered a great loss. Notice that justice works equally to all. Balaam was put to death when Joshua brought the people into the land. The enemy doesn't appear to have any new plans. He doesn't have to make new ones because the Lord's people tend to fall for the old ones in each generation. Do not make this mistake. Remain steadfast in your commitment to serve the Lord and avoid needless pain brought on you by deceptive people.

2. PHYSICAL

Therefore God also gave them up to uncleanness, in the lusts of their hearts, to dishonor their bodies among themselves, who exchanged the truth of God for the lie, and worshiped and served the creature rather than the Creator, who is blessed forever. Amen. (Romans 1:24-25)

Uncleanness may be a sign that you have been given up by the Lord to the condition you have chosen. I don't know about you, but I know with certainty that I do not want this to be said of me. Notice that this condition leaves people without the assistance of the truth of God. They are living according to the lies of the enemy and are moving further and further away from the Lord. I like the idea of trading up rather than trading down. The people referenced in the passage above made a terrible trade. They exchanged the truth for a lie. In spiritual ignorance, they began to worship the creature rather than the creator. The loss for them is unimaginable. The writer of the book of Romans warns us that the same thing can happen to us if we don't hold onto the truth and guard it with our lives.

In the passage below, notice that touching unclean things in the natural has the potential to make us unclean and guilty in the spiritual realm. We must guard against touching unclean things if we want to remain close to the Lord. These things can leave us in the spiritual condition of being guilty before the Lord. If there is any root of this in us, we need to come to the Lord for cleansing. Why is this so important? We must be cleansed to draw close to Him and receive the indwelling of the Holy Spirit.

> Or if a person touches any unclean thing, whether it is the carcass of an unclean beast, or the carcass of unclean livestock, or the carcass of unclean creeping things, and he is unaware of it, he also shall be unclean and guilty. Or if he touches human unclean-ness—whatever uncleanness with which a man may be defiled, and he is unaware of it—when he realizes it, then he shall be guilty. (Leviticus 5:2-3)

3. SOUL

(Our emotions, will, reasoning and decision making)

For God did not call us to uncleanness, but in holiness. Therefore he who rejects this does not reject man, but God, who has also given us His Holy Spirit. (1 Thessalonians 4:7-8)

Notice that the Lord has called us in holiness, and expects us to respond in holiness. Rejecting this calling and remaining in an unclean state means that we have rejected God. It means that we have rejected the one who has given us His Holy Spirit. If you or others you know have been led away from the Lord, we lift all of you up in prayer right now. May your spiritual ears be opened once again for you to see your redemption drawing nigh and to hear the call of the Lord! He is releasing this call once again in the passage below. Can you hear Him calling to you to come out from among the unclean and worldly people around you? This is another invitation to accept the Lord as your Father. Will you always choose Him?

Therefore "Come out from among them and be separate," says the Lord. "Do not touch what is unclean, and I will receive you." "I will be a Father to you, and you shall be My sons and daughters," says the Lord Almighty. (2 Corinthians 6:17-18)

In the passage below from the book of Leviticus, the Lord asks people to go to the priest who has been authorized to make atonement for them. Some people ignore this passage from the Torah because they don't have a Levitical Priest to whom they can turn. The good news is that we do have an eternal high priest who has already worked our atonement for us. Amen? Remember Hebrews 9:14, "...*how much more shall the blood of Christ, who through the eternal Spirit offered Himself without spot to God, cleanse your conscience from dead works to serve the living God?*" Our High Priest, Yeshua ha Messiach, has once and for all made atonement for us. As you read the passage below from Leviticus, remember who your priest is right now. Turn to Him and ask Him to make atonement for you right now. Amen?

> *Then the priest shall make atonement on his behalf before the Lord: the priest shall offer the sin offering, to make atonement for the one to be cleansed from his uncleanness.* (Leviticus 14:19)

DAVID'S COMMITMENT TO THE LORD

> *I will set nothing wicked before my eyes; I hate the work of those who fall away; it shall not cling to me. A perverse heart shall depart from me; I will not know wickedness.* (Psalm 101:3-4)

Like Job, David made a commitment to the Lord which he intended to keep. To do this David knew that he needed to be clean in the Lord's eyes. The Lord promises something better for those who want to remain free from wickedness.

The Lord saves us from all uncleanness. This is such a wonderful promise. Think about it. We have an awesome God, and He always works for our good. He desires to be close to us. He wants to abide in the Temple which is in our hearts. Then He does all the hard work of cleansing the temple so He can live there within us. Hallelujah! The Lord is good all the time! Amen?

ACTIVATION

We look again to David to see how he activated the Lord's promises in his life and service for the Kingdom of God. Most of his prayers were lifted up to the Lord during very difficult times. In most cases, David's life was in danger as he prayed. Notice that he intentionally chose not to look to people for help. He had experienced betrayal, resistance, and rebellion from his people as well as from his own family and friends. He quickly learned that the Lord was the only one he could count on. So he developed a process and plan. He always turned to the Lord when he needed help, forgiveness, and cleansing.

Each time he was faced with trouble, David turned to the Lord in prayer. He began by acknowledging who the Lord is, what He has done in the past, and what he is doing right now. Then he gave the Lord all his praise and worship. He lifted Him up in worship and gave Him the glory that is due to His holy name. Only then did he claim the promise and make his request to the Lord. Think about it. Most of the time his prayer process began when he named one of the Lord's promises.

David looked at something specific the Lord had released to him in a promise, and then he placed a claim on that promise. Next, by faith, David activated the Lord's promises in his life. The Word of God gives this account of David's prayers to us as an example for us to follow. Which promise of the Lord do you need most right now? Look it up in the Bible and when the time is right speak it exactly as it is given. Speak it aloud several times and believe that it is yours. This will activate it in your life as it did in David's life. Don't forget to give the Lord your praise and thanksgiving as you end this process.

PREPARING FOR ACTIVATION

Many times repentance is needed to prepare people for a season of cleansing. It is important to rid ourselves of the roadblocks which make it difficult for the Lord to work in our lives. The Lord has allowed us to participate in this very important process of removing all our uncleanness. He does not want us to feel like helpless victims even when we need to go through the process of the forgiveness of sin and cleansing of our souls. We are invited to be the initiators of our cleansing process. Is it time for you to take action to open a way for the Lord to do a mighty work in your spirit, soul, and body? Start by praying the prayer in the passage below.

> *Have mercy upon me, O God, according to Your*
> *lovingkindness; according to the multitude of Your*
> *tender mercies, blot out my transgressions. Wash me*
> *thoroughly from my iniquity, and cleanse me from*
> *my sin. For I acknowledge my transgressions, and*
> *my sin is always before me.* (Psalm 51:1-3)

The passage above is how King David began the process of His cleansing. His sin was great and David needed a powerful and thorough cleansing. Read that prayer aloud several times until it becomes your prayer as it reflects the state of readiness in your own heart. After his repentance, David focused once again on the character of God and asked Him to respond out of His integrity and His commitment to the truth to invade every part of David's being. He asked the Lord to deal with parts of his inner being which were unknown to him. We all have a blind spot and need help to make it clear and then deal with it. David is trusting the Lord to deal with his inner desires which tempt him to sin.

> *Behold, You desire truth in the inward parts, and in*
> *the hidden part You will make me to know wisdom.*
> *Purge me with hyssop, and I shall be clean; wash me,*
> *and I shall be whiter than snow. Make me hear joy*
> *and gladness, that the bones You have broken may*
> *rejoice. Hide Your face from my sins, and blot out*
> *all my iniquities.* (Psalm 51:6-9)

It appears that David is asking the Lord's help to deal with this problem in the depth of his being. He is calling on the

Lord to do more than just merely cleaning up one mess in his life. David is asking the Lord's help to heal all his uncleanness and to restore him to a state of righteousness before the Lord. Many times when people say they have no sin, they also have a large area of unknowing in their spirit and soul. Only the Lord can reveal what we have hidden from ourselves. To be ready to activate this process in your life, I urge you to take it to the Lord and allow the Spirit of truth to reveal what you need to know for you to receive all you need to make a huge change. Remember that the Holy Spirit can guide you into all truth when you are ready and willing to receive it.

> *I still have many things to say to you, but you cannot bear them now. However, when He, the Spirit of truth, has come, He will guide you into all truth; for He will not speak on His own authority, but whatever He hears He will speak; and He will tell you things to come. (John 16:12-13)*

PRAYERS

> *O God, my heart is steadfast; I will sing and give praise, even with my glory. Awake, lute and harp! I will awaken the dawn. I will praise You, O Lord, among the peoples, and I will sing praises to You among the nations. For Your mercy is great above the heavens, and Your truth reaches to the clouds. Be exalted, O God, above the heavens, and Your glory above all the earth; that Your beloved may*

be delivered, save with Your right hand, and hear me. God has spoken in His holiness: "I will rejoice; I will divide Shechem and measure out the Valley of Succoth. Gilead is Mine; Manasseh is Mine; Ephraim also is the helmet for My head; Judah is My lawgiver. Moab is My washpot; over Edom I will cast My shoe; over Philistia I will triumph." (Psalm 108:1-9)

Give us help from trouble, for the help of man is useless. Through God we will do valiantly, for it is He who shall tread down our enemies. (Psalm 108:12-13)

ACTIVATION

This is a reminder for you. I want to give you a summary of what we have been looking at in the pages above. It is a good time to look again at David to see how he activated the Lord's promises in his life and service for the Kingdom of God. All these prayers were lifted up to the Lord during very difficult times. In most cases, David's life was in danger as he prayed. He didn't look to people for help. He always turned to the Lord. Each time, he acknowledged who the Lord is and what he does before activating His promises. Notice how he does this in the first prayer above.

SELAH QUESTIONS

(Selah means to pause and meditate on these things.)

1. What did you experience when you worked through the review at the beginning of this chapter?

_____

_____

_____

2. Have you asked the Holy Spirit to reveal to you things that need cleansing in your heart?

_____

_____

_____

3. Why do you think the Lord speaks these promises over and over?

_____

_____

_____

4. What three areas in your life need cleansing and healing?

_____

_____

_____

5. What kind of covenant did Job and David make with the Lord?

_____

_____

_____

6. How are you moving to activate these promises in your life and work?

_____

_____

_____

CHAPTER SEVEN

Promise Six

I Will Summon the Grain

"I will summon the grain and increase it"
(Ezekiel 36:29b)

When I speak at conferences and mention restoration and increase, people tend to get very excited. They quickly line up filled with hope because they want to receive it by impartation right away. Compare this with the process we have been looking at in this book. I am asking you to make this comparison at this time to prepare yourself to receive the full restoration and increase promised by the Lord. This process is not always as popular as the thrill of receiving an impartation from the Lord. The word the Lord gave through Ezekiel made it clear that five steps needed to be completed before the people were fully prepared to receive promises six and seven. Our generation wants its benefits immediately with no delays or steps to follow. I am convinced that the Lord wants us to move through this process step by step so that He can prepare us to receive more. Remember that He is able and willing to give us more than we can imagine. Consider again the passage of scripture below:

> Now to Him who is able to do exceedingly abundantly above all that we ask or think, according to the power that works in us, to Him be glory in the church by Christ Jesus to all generations, forever and ever. Amen. (Ephesians 3:20-21)

For greater clarity on what the Lord is promising to us, I recommend that you read the entire promise again. "*I will summon the grain and increase it, and not send famine against you.*" (Ezekiel 36:29b, CJB) The Lord promises to give you what you need to thrive and not merely survive. Then He plans to give you more. He promises to give you increase on the abundance you have already received. But this isn't the end of the promise. He goes one more step and promises to protect your abundance from loss. Remember what Yeshua promised in John 10:10, "*The thief does not come except to steal, and to kill, and to destroy. I have come that they may have life, and that they may have it more abundantly.*" I like the promise of Yeshua for us to have life more abundantly. How about you?

To make it abundantly clear, let's go through the promise again and look at it from a different angle. As noted above, there are three elements to this promise. Two are positive and the third is in the form of a negative statement. The Lord promises to bring in the grain needed to feed His people. He also begins the amazing process of giving us a continuous increase. He also affirms that the grain and the increase will be protected from things that may try to take them away. I believe that the promised protection is greater than just the possibility of a future time of famine. The Lord summed up this promise for another generation in the passage below. At the same time, the Lord has extended these same promises to us in our generation.

> And try Me now in this, says the Lord of hosts, "If I will not open for you the windows of heaven and pour out for you such blessing that there will not be room enough to receive it. And I will rebuke the devourer for your sakes, So that he will not destroy the fruit of your ground, nor shall the vine fail to bear fruit for you in the field," says the Lord of hosts; (Malachi 3:10b-11)

In Genesis, Chapter 26 the Lord released the same sevenfold blessing to Isaac which He had previously given to Abraham. All that the Lord had promised and all He had done in the past for Abraham was now going to be done for and given to his son Isaac. The Lord always passes His promises and blessings to the next generation. To confirm this, look again at Psalm 115:14, "May the Lord give you increase more and more, you and your children." This is one of my favorite blessings in the Psalms. I want all my blessings to be passed to my children. How about you?

As I celebrated the goodness of the Lord and read more in Genesis Chapter 26, I found seven more powerful and amazing "I will" promises of the Lord for provision and protection. These were all being passed down to Isaac. I became convinced that the Lord's promises become new and more powerful for each new generation. As you study these promises, don't forget to read them aloud as you receive them and activate them for yourself in this generation. In Genesis 26:25-26, the Lord gives the remaining two promises to Isaac. This passage is available for you a little further down in this section. If you are unfamiliar with the names and places as spoken in Hebrew, look at the "Glossary of Hebrew Names and Terms" at the end of this chapter.

> *A famine came over the land, not the same as the first famine which had taken place when Avraham was alive. Yitz'chak (Isaac) went to G'rar, to Avimelech king of the P'lishtim. Adonai appeared to him and said: "Don't go down into Egypt, but live where I tell you. Stay in this land, and __I will__ be with you and bless you, because, __I will__ give all these lands to you and to your descendants. __I will__ fulfill the oath which I swore to Avraham your father – __I will__ make your descendants as numerous as the stars in the sky, __I will__ give all these lands to your descendants, and by your descendants all the nations of the earth will bless themselves. All this is because Avraham heeded what I said and did what I told him to do – he followed my mitzvot, my regulations and my teachings."* (Genesis 26:1-5, CJB)

Think about this: Isaac was not Father God's grandson. He was just as much a child of God as his father Abraham. The Lord loves each of us because we are His children. We are not called into a relationship with Him through our parents. In the same way, our children are not related to the Father as grandchildren. They are as much His children as you and I. The important thing for us to realize is that we have a calling and an invitation from Father God to have our full status as His children. Each of us has a promised inheritance that comes directly from Him rather than a limited inheritance from our natural parents. Whoever you are in this world, you are a son or daughter of the Living God in the spiritual realm.

Just as Isaac received the same promises which his father Abraham had received, you have an inheritance just like theirs. Galatians 3:13-14, "*Christ has redeemed us from the curse of the law, having become a curse for us (for it is written, "Cursed is everyone who hangs on a tree"), that the blessing of Abraham might come upon the Gentiles in Christ Jesus, that we might receive the promise of the Spirit through faith.*" The inheritance is yours whether you are Jew or Gentile, male or female or rich or poor. We are all considered the same in the eyes of the Lord. It is time for each of us to claim our inheritance and activate it.

As I mentioned earlier, the passage from Genesis 26 above only lists five promises rather than the seven I referenced earlier. Another message from the Lord is in this chapter. Think about what the Lord is doing by listing the promises in two stages. You will see here another common theme with the Lord. He tends to release powerful promises and gifts partially at first. Then as we begin to receive and activate them, He gives more. The Lord gave the "promised land" to the Children of Israel in stages, because they were not large enough to occupy all of it when they moved in. This was an act of mercy. If a sparse populace occupied the land, wild animals would have increased and then attacked the people. As their numbers increased, He gave them more. Think about what this means for you and me. The Lord is also patient to give us more as we are ready to receive it. The remaining two promises were reserved for the last part of chapter 26.

> From there Yitz'chak went up to Be'er-sheva. Adonai appeared to him that same night and said, "**I am** the God of Avraham your father. Don't be afraid, because **I am** with you; <u>**I will**</u> bless you and (**I will**) increase your descendants for the sake of my servant Avraham." There he built an altar and called on the name of Adonai. He pitched his tent there; and there Yitz'chak's servants dug a well. (Genesis 26:23-25, CJB)

Notice how Isaac responded to the Lord's promise. He first assumed by faith that all of the promises were true. He received them in gratitude and stood in faith waiting for their fulfillment. Then he built an altar. He gave praise to the Lord before anything manifested in his life. The third thing He did was to call upon the name of Adonai (the God of mercy). Finally, Isaac and his followers took an action step. They dug a well. If you expect to receive great blessings from the Lord, demonstrate your faith by beginning to build something to hold them. Take some action on your own. If you expect to receive a powerful flow of living water, dig a well. Amen?

The main thing I want you to receive right now is a pure and full experience of an ever-increasing faith in the Lord. Trust me you can trust the Lord. He has always demonstrated Himself to be worthy of our trust. Now consider this: The Lord released these promises over and over in the past and He will release them to you as well when you become ready to receive them. The central idea at this point is that He is releasing them once more for you and me. Would you like to hear the Lord promising you INCREASE? Take hold of the promise in Psalm 115 once again and continue to make it yours.

> *The Lord has been mindful of us; He will bless us; He will bless the house of Israel; He will bless the house of Aaron. He will bless those who fear the Lord, both small and great. May the Lord give you increase more and more, you and your children. May you be blessed by the Lord, Who made heaven and earth.* (Psalm 115:12-15)

This is exactly what He is doing now. In this generation, He is blessing you and me. Besides, as we faithfully obey and serve Him, He is giving us increase more and more. He has promised to extend this blessing to the next generation. Our children will also receive more and more from the Lord. I like increase. How about you? This is a good time to receive all these promises and blessings, activate them in faith, and let the Lord do more and more for you, your children, and your spiritual children. Amen?

THE LORD KEPT HIS PROMISE

Yitz'chak planted crops in that land and reaped that year a hundred times as much as he had sowed. Adonai had blessed him. (Genesis 26:12, CJB)

I look at this as a promise released, a promise received and a promise activated. It doesn't matter what your circumstances are. Nothing is impossible for the Lord. Think about it. There was a famine in the land. No one was sowing seeds, because they would simply wilt and die in the dry soil. However, Isaac was living by faith and not by his circumstances. In the middle of a famine, he sowed in faith and then reaped one hundredfold. I believe the Lord wants to release this same promise along with all this increase now for you. Are you ready to receive it and activate it with your faith?

It is so simple. All we have to do is receive it and activate the promise! Begin now to speak the promises aloud. Believe the Lord's word. He keeps all his promises. He did it then and He will do it now. Claim it for yourself and your children. Speak it aloud by saying: The Lord will give me increase! Say it over and over until it manifests in your heart. This is not a one-time deal. Keep speaking the powerful and trustworthy word of God. He has done it over and over throughout history and He will do it for you.

It is important to understand that giving is part of God's character. His character is changeless. Each generation needs to receive and activate the promises. Now it is your turn. Receive the blessing in Psalm 115 once again at a deeper level. Speak it over yourself and speak it over others: "*May the Lord give you increase more and more, you and your children. May you be blessed by the Lord, Who made heaven and earth*" (Psalm 115:14-15). Are you getting it? Did you receive it? Then keep praying it over and over as you release it to all the people around you today.

SUMMON THE GRAIN

As I worked on this chapter, I was invited to speak at a conference. As I shared this message with the people, my mind began to ponder this promise more fully. I wondered how this promise would look when it manifested. I tried to imagine it, but the images seemed funny rather than revelatory. As I stood in front of the people teaching this lesson, I went into an open vision. In the vision, I saw a field of fully developed corn move into the courtyard of the church. The field of corn appeared to plant itself. As I looked at the corn, I saw that it was fully ripe and ready for harvest. What an awesome Father God. I thought to myself: This is the fullness of the blessing.

> *I will also save you from all your uncleannesses: and I will call for the corn, and will increase it, and lay no famine upon you.* (Ezekiel 36:29, KJV)

I suddenly felt very comforted in my spirit. The Lord doesn't do things halfway. He didn't send some seed I needed to plant and then wait for a long time for the harvest. I didn't need to plow, pick weeds, or water the crop. The corn came fully ready to be harvested immediately. I quickly understood that my vision was not about a crop of corn in the natural. The Lord was pointing to the spiritual harvest time in which the believers in our generation have been called to be kingdom harvesters. Then I thought about something Yeshua once said.

> Do you not say, 'There are still four months and then comes the harvest'? Behold, I say to you, lift up your eyes and look at the fields, for they are already white for harvest! And he who reaps receives wages, and gathers fruit for eternal life, that both he who sows and he who reaps may rejoice together. (John 4:35-36)

The vision reminded me that it is harvest time right now. We are not just praying for harvest while we spend our time looking years ahead for it to manifest. It is already here. It was true when Yeshua spoke it to the disciples and it is true for you and me. As I listen to people speaking about the end time harvest, they seem to speak of it as a future event. It is as if we are slowly preparing now for something to come much later. This is not what Yeshua said. We need to look and see that the fields are already ripe for harvest. Can you see it? I like the idea that harvest time will be a season for us to rejoice together as we see the lost being found in the Lord.

THE GRAIN

And He said to them, "Do you not understand this parable? How then will you understand all the parables? The sower sows the word. (Mark 4:13-14)

I believe the grain in this promise represents something spiritual as well as something in the natural. I believe the Lord is promising to give us everything we need to be effective in the harvest. He is promising to provide more than enough and then to keep increasing it to meet every need which may arise. My clue for this spiritual reality was revealed by Yeshua in the passage below. To see the spiritual meaning of this promise, we need to look at the grain as the Word of God. The Lord gives it to us to enable us to plant and harvest in season. The Word is once again being sent out to the lost so they may be saved before it is too late. Amen?

Most of us like the idea of increase. I know I do and I pray for it all the time. I release it now to you as part of the Lord's promises and plans for your life. Begin by believing that He will give you all you need to accomplish your purpose and reach your destiny in the Kingdom of God. Remember that abundant provision comes to us with a purpose. It is to build us up and sustain us during the season of harvest. The Lord is so gracious that He provides a prayer of impartation for us in His Word. I pray this prayer of increase for you in the passage below. Now it is your turn to pray it over those in your area of ministry.

Now may He who supplies seed to the sower, and bread for food, supply and multiply the seed you have sown and increase the fruits of your righteousness, while you are enriched in everything for all liberality, which causes thanksgiving through us to God. For the administration of this service not only supplies the needs of the saints, but also is abounding through many thanksgivings to God, while, through the proof of this ministry, they glorify God for the obedience of your confession to the gospel of Christ, and for your liberal sharing with them and all men, and by their prayer for you, who long for you because of the exceeding grace of God in you. Thanks be to God for His indescribable gift! (2 Corinthians 9:10-15)

As I mentioned above, the Lord is a giver and you and I have been made in His image. We are destined to be givers like our Father in Heaven. He provides an abundance so that we can give more. Also, he plans to provide for our needs and the righteous desires of our hearts. It is appropriate for us to feast now on the provision of the Lord which is being released to us just as He promised. As we receive His amazing gifts we are prepared for increase and not decrease. In the passage below, you will find another promise of the Lord which is likely very familiar to you. I give it here so that you can not only receive it but also activate it in your life and ministry.

For I know the plans I have for you," declares the Lord, "plans to prosper you and not to harm you, plans to give you hope and a future. Then you will call upon

me and come and pray to me, and I will listen to you.
You will seek me and find me when you seek me with
all your heart. (Jeremiah 29:11-13, NIV)

We are blessed to be living in one of the Lord's great seasons of restoration. In Ezekiel 39, the Lord explains that He does this for two reasons. He restores the things which belong to His people. Why? It is because He is good all the time and He is concerned about the welfare of His people. Remember He does it to bring glory to His name. Too many people have disrespected and robbed the name of God of the glory He deserves. The Lord is jealous for His holy name and will do what it takes to restore it in the eyes of everyone on earth.

Therefore thus says the Lord God: Now I will restore
the fortunes of Jacob and have mercy on the whole
house of Israel, and I will be jealous for my holy
name. They shall forget their shame and all the
treachery they have practiced against me, when they
dwell securely in their land with none to make them
afraid, when I have brought them back from the peo-
ples and gathered them from their enemies' lands,
and through them have vindicated my holiness in
the sight of many nations. (Ezekiel 39:25-27, ESV)

ACTIVATION

Another great activation prayer by David is given in Psalm 145:1-9. As you receive these powerful promises of God, work to improve your skills at activating each one just as David did in the prayers. David shows us another great way to receive and activate the promises of God. In this lesson please notice that praise is the main key to activating the promises. Praise releases the power inherent in each of the Lord's amazing promises. Prepare now for a fresh new activation. Pray these prayers aloud over yourself, your family, and your ministry. Amen?

> *I will extol You, my God, O King; and I will bless Your name forever and ever. Every day I will bless You, and I will praise Your name forever and ever. Great is the Lord, and greatly to be praised; and His greatness is unsearchable. One generation shall praise Your works to another, and shall declare Your mighty acts. I will meditate on the glorious splendor of Your majesty, and on Your wondrous works. Men shall speak of the might of Your awesome acts, and I will declare Your greatness. They shall utter the memory of Your great goodness, and shall sing of Your righteousness. The Lord is gracious and full of compassion, slow to anger and great in mercy. The Lord is good to all, and His tender mercies are over all His works. (Psalm 145:1-9)*

Remember our lesson above found in the twenty-sixth chapter of the book of Genesis. The Lord released the same sevenfold blessing to Isaac which He had given to Abraham. Seven speaks of fullness or completeness. The Lord was not offering a small portion of the blessing, but the fullness to

Isaac. Think about it. Isaac was going to receive the fullness of the blessing of Abraham. All that the Lord had promised and done for His friend Abraham was now given to his son Isaac. In that chapter, I found seven "I will" promises of the Lord which were being extended to Abraham's son, Isaac. As I said earlier in this chapter, these same promises are now available to you and me through the completed work of Yeshua ha Messiach. Notice that the Psalmist also referenced the extension of these blessings to all of the Lord's people.

PRAYER

But You, O Lord, are a shield for me, my glory and the One who lifts up my head. I cried to the Lord with my voice, and He heard me from His holy hill. Selah I lay down and slept; I awoke, for the Lord sustained me. I will not be afraid of ten thousands of people who have set themselves against me all around. Arise, O Lord; Save me, O my God! For You have struck all my enemies on the cheekbone; You have broken the teeth of the ungodly. Salvation belongs to the Lord. Your blessing is upon Your people. (Psalm 3:3-8, CJB)

SELAH QUESTIONS

(Selah means to pause and meditate on these things.)

1. Are you willing to do whatever it takes to prepare yourself to receive the promises of the Lord?

_____

_____

_____

2. What are the three elements in this promise from the Lord?

_____

_____

_____

3. Do you believe these promises are for you? Why?

_____

_____

_____

4. How did Isaac respond to receiving these promises from the Lord?

_____

_____

_____

5. How did the Lord confirm this promise in the life and work of Isaac?

_____

_____

_____

6. What do you think it will look like when the Lord releases this promise for you?

_____

_____

_____

7. What are you doing for the Lord in this great harvest season?

_____

_____

_____

GLOSSARY OF HEBREW NAMES AND TERMS

Avraham	Abraham
Yitz'chak	Isaac
G'rar	Gerar
Avimelech	Abimelech a Philistine King
P'lishtim	Philistines
Mitzvoth	Mitzvah – righteous acts which go beyond mere requirements
Be'er-sheva	Beersheba: the ancient home of Abraham and his descendants

CHAPTER EIGHT

Promise Seven

I Will Multiply Your Fruit

I will multiply the yield of fruit from the trees and increase production in the fields, so that you never again suffer the reproach of famine among the nations. (Ezekiel 36:30)

As we studied lesson seven, I asked you to notice how the Lord chooses to do math? Over and over, He has demonstrated that He prefers to do multiplication rather than simple addition for His children. I noticed that there is one particular promise He appears to release to generation after generation. This promise is summed up in the words He spoke to Abraham. *"For when God made a promise to Abraham, because He could swear by no one greater, He swore by Himself, saying, 'Surely blessing I will bless you, and multiplying I will multiply you.'"* (Hebrews 6:13-14) The Lord promised to bless His people in every generation. Consider the promise personally. He plans to give you more than you need so that you can give to others in need. Then He adds the amazing and wonderful promise to multiply all these blessings.

As I read this promise over and over, I began to notice something special about our Father God. It was the two words "*and multiplying*" which caught my attention. In this simple statement, the Lord lets us know that it is His nature to continuously multiply the blessings He has already promised. After He has given His blessings to His people, He multiplies them more and more. It was not merely done for a few people once or twice in the past. It is not a one-time deal. It is a part of the Lord's character to be continuously multiplying His love and blessings for His people. In your relationship with the Father, believe, receive, and activate the Lord's multiplication promise for you and your family. Let Him increase more and more all the good gifts He has already graciously given to you. Also, allow Him to multiply all He has given to your family and ministry. You can trust Him. This is who He is and this is what He does. It is both in His nature and in His plan for you. Amen?

Now ask yourself once again: How would you like to activate this promise of multiplication in your life and ministry? Remember you don't have to beg Him to do what He has already promised to do. All you have to do is receive it by faith and then activate it in your life and ministry. Begin now to receive this awesome promise from the Lord. This is a good time to say aloud: He will multiply the fruit in my life! Keep saying it until you believe it with all your spirit and mind. I

don't know about you, but I like the Lord's math. When He
is giving out blessings, favor, provision, protection, and revelation, I always want Him to multiply these wonderful gifts
for me. How about you?

SHABBAT AND MANNA

The Lord began to reveal this aspect of His character (multiplication) to another generation as the children of Israel
departed from Egypt. He revealed to His people this process slowly and systematically as He made known His character attributes and His appointed times (*moadim*). (For an
explanation of the Hebrew words used, check the Glossary
of Hebrew names and words at the end of this chapter.) The
First appointed time the Lord gave to His people was the seventh day of rest which He called "Shabbat". When He began
to feed the people with manna (the bread from heaven), they
were told to only collect a one day supply of two omers per
person. They were not to keep any of it overnight.

Of course, some of them tested the Lord and kept it until the
next day. To their shock, it was rotten and filled with worms.
This was a visible sign which manifested because they had disobeyed the Lord. As the day of Shabbat drew near, the Lord
gave the first step in multiplication. They were not to work on
Shabbat. So the Lord let the sixth day supply of manna remain
good through the seventh day. He did this by doubling the
manna so they had something to eat on Shabbat. On Shabbat,
the amount kept overnight did not rot or have worms. This

was a great revelation of the Lord's provision and protection over the children of Israel, and it is a sign for us as well. The Lord knew before we did, that at times we need a double portion of His provision. He had already made His plan and they received what they needed. In the same way, we will receive what we need (and more) when the Lord releases His attribute of multiplication again for our generation.

> *And so it was, on the sixth day, that they gathered twice as much bread, two omers for each one. And all the rulers of the congregation came and told Moses. Then he said to them, "This is what the Lord has said: 'Tomorrow is a Sabbath rest, a holy Sabbath to the Lord. Bake what you will bake today, and boil what you will boil; and lay up for yourselves all that remains, to be kept until morning.'" So they laid it up till morning, as Moses commanded; and it did not stink, nor were there any worms in it. Then Moses said, "Eat that today, for today is a Sabbath to the Lord; today you will not find it in the field. Six days you shall gather it, but on the seventh day, the Sabbath, there will be none." (Exodus 16:22-26)*

It would be nice if this part of the story ended at this point, but some of the people tested the Lord again. Testing the Lord is never a good idea and as you might expect it didn't go well for them. As some people went out to gather manna on Shabbat, they broke two commandments. First, they were told not to gather any of it on Shabbat, but they didn't trust the Lord's promise of provision. The second commandment they broke was given to Moses on the mountain. They were told to do no work on Shabbat. But they threw caution to the wind and disobeyed right before His eyes. The Lord spoke to Moses about His disappointment with the people's behavior and restated the promise of double portions being released on the sixth day.

> Now it happened that some of the people went out on the seventh day to gather, but they found none. And the Lord said to Moses, "How long do you refuse to keep My commandments and My laws? See! For the Lord has given you the Sabbath; therefore He gives you on the sixth day bread for two days. Let every man remain in his place; let no man go out of his place on the seventh day." So the people rested on the seventh day. (Exodus 16:27-30)

Shabbat Year (Shmita or Shemittah)

The Lord demonstrated this process of multiplication for Moses and the children of Israel powerfully during the time of their exodus from Egypt. He told the people not to plant crops during the seventh year. The seventh year was to be something like a yearlong Shabbat for the land. It was a time for the land to rest as the Lord refreshed and renewed the soil. The faith challenge was to trust that Father God would feed them while the soil was resting. The Lord proved to them that He and His promises were both trustworthy. Then He used the process of multiplication to give them all the provision they needed.

> *Whatever the land yields during the sabbath year will be food for you—for yourself, your manservant and maidservant, and the hired worker and temporary resident who live among you, as well as for your livestock and the wild animals in your land. Whatever the land produces may be eaten.* (Leviticus 25:6-7, NIV)

Even though they did not sow, the Lord provided enough volunteer grain to feed them for a year. That is a lot of grain. Amen? He provided so much that it fed a multitude of people and animals. The farmer, his servants, his hired workers, the temporary residents in the land, the livestock, and the wild animals all had enough to eat. I don't know about you, but that sounds like a lot of multiplication to me. Every living thing would have food to eat during the Lord's Shmita. We are reminded once more that the Lord keeps His promises. He can provide for you in the worst of times. Not one of His promises will fail for those who put their trust in Him. Amen?

JUBILEE YEAR

The Lord made another amazing promise for those who would trust and obey. He added to His promise by giving more than a double portion. He said that He would triple the crops in the sixth year when it was time for the Yovel (Jubilee). Think about this: there would be no crops sown during the seventh year. When the next year was the Yovel, no crops would be sown that year either. The year after Yovel, they had to wait until harvest time to bring in their food. This would mean no crops for almost three years. The Lord did His multiplication so there would be plenty for them to eat.

> *And if you say, "What shall we eat in the seventh year, since we shall not sow nor gather in our produce?" Then I will command My blessing on you in the sixth year, and it will bring forth produce enough for three years. And you shall sow in the eighth year, and eat old produce until the ninth year; until its produce comes in, you shall eat of the old harvest.* (Leviticus 25:20-22)

The crops of the sixth year would feed them during the sixth year, the seventh year, the eighth year, and carry over into the first year of a new cycle until new crops could be planted and harvested. The Lord kept all of His promises and in the process, He also continued to help them by increasing their faith. In the two passages below, notice how the Lord explained it to them. This was not just for them. Think about it: this promise is also for you. As you look ahead at potential shortages during seasons of famine, pestilence, and the destructive forces of nature (flooding, tornados, hurricanes, etc.), put your faith in God. He can and will miraculously provide for you in all of the circumstances which affect your life.

DOUBLE PORTION RESTORATION

*Return to the stronghold, you prisoners of hope. Even today I declare that **I will restore double** to you. For I have bent Judah, My bow, fitted the bow with Ephraim, and raised up your sons, O Zion, against your sons, O Greece, and made you like the sword of a mighty man." Then the Lord will be seen over them, and His arrow will go forth like lightning. The Lord God will blow the trumpet, and go with whirlwinds from the south. The Lord of hosts will defend them; They shall devour and subdue with slingstones. They shall drink and roar as if with wine; They shall be filled with blood like basins, like the corners of the altar. The Lord their God will save them in that day, as the flock of His people. For they shall be like the jewels of a crown, lifted like a banner over His land—* (Zechariah 9:12-16)

Restoration is always a good thing. Double portion restoration is even better. The Lord gave this same double portion restoration to Job after his time of testing was over. "*And the Lord **restored Job's** losses when he prayed for his friends. Indeed the Lord gave Job **twice as much** as he had before.*" (Job 42:10) Here is a thought. Notice what the Lord did not double. He did not double his wife or his children. All of these people had been a spiritual burden for Job. Here is some good news. The Lord doesn't give double trouble to His faithful children. Now, notice that the Lord released this same promise again in the generation of Isaiah.

*Instead of their shame my people will receive a double portion, and instead of disgrace they will rejoice in their inheritance; and so **they will inherit a double portion** in their land, and everlasting joy will be theirs.* (**Isaiah** 61:7)

Generation after generation the Lord has kept promising double portion (or more) to His people. Remember that the Lord keeps His word. David and Joshua both declared that the Lord had kept all His promises released in their generations. They increased the emphasis by saying, "Not one of His promises failed." Now it is your time to receive it. As you prepare to receive the promise and activate it, notice that the Lord released the promise again through the prophet Zechariah. He said, "*Return to the stronghold, you prisoners of hope. Even today I declare that **I will restore double to you**.* (Zechariah 9:12) This double portion blessing is common to every generation. It is now being released to you. Are you ready to believe it, receive it, and activate it?

FRUIT

The Lord's choice of fruit to explain this promise is enlightening and encouraging. The word, fruit, has more than one meaning. We immediately think of the fruit growing on trees, and it is evident that this is one of the main meanings of the word. But as I spent time meditating on His promises, I began to be convinced that the Lord meant more than just food. Then I was led to the two verses below. I pray that they will also give you a revelation of the Lord's plan in your life and ministry.

1. FRUIT OF THE SPIRIT

> *But the fruit of the Spirit is love, joy, peace, long-suffering, kindness, goodness, faithfulness, gentleness, self-control. Against such there is no law.* (Galatians 5:22-23)

The promises of the Lord are not just for the natural realm. He also provides and multiplies His provision for us in the spiritual realm. I believe that the Lord feeds us with the fruit resulting from everything we do for His kingdom as we exercise the spiritual gifts He has released to us. Remember what Yeshua said in John 4:32, "*But He said to them, 'I have food to eat of which you do not know.'*" The disciples had no idea what He was talking about. So He explained it to them. "*Jesus said to them, "My food is to do the will of Him who sent Me, and to finish His work."* (John 4:34) Paul makes clear the difference between the fruit of the Spirit and the unfruitful works of darkness in the passage below.

> *For you were once darkness, but now you are light in the Lord. Walk as children of light (for the fruit of the Spirit is in all goodness, righteousness, and truth), finding out what is acceptable to the Lord. And have no fellowship with the unfruitful works of darkness, but rather expose them.* (Ephesians 5:8-11)

2. FRUIT OF OUR LABORS (in the harvest)

Therefore be patient, brethren, until the coming of the Lord. See how the farmer waits for the precious fruit of the earth, waiting patiently for it until it receives the early and latter rain. You also be patient. Establish your hearts, for the coming of the Lord is at hand. (James 5:7-8)

Yeshua often used illustrations of processes in the natural to explain the things of the Kingdom of God. Back in those days, everyone could identify with the work of a farmer. Just as a farmer waits patiently for the well-watered crops to manifest, a Kingdom worker should also learn patience. Stand fast in your faith. Remember that the coming of the Lord is at hand. Be about His business until He returns. In one of His parables, Yeshua said, "*So he called ten of his servants, delivered to them ten minas, and said to them,* (Luke 19:13). [In the context of the great harvest, the Lord is saying the same thing to us.] "*Do business till I come (Luke 19:13b)*." For you and me, this means for us to be patient and produce fruit for the Kingdom by bringing the lost souls back to the Father's family.

3. FRUIT OF RIGHTEOUSNESS

Now the fruit of righteousness is sown in peace by those who make peace. (James 3:18)

The Word of God speaks of the fruit of righteousness over and over. As I reflected on this word, I started to wonder: Am I producing the fruit of righteousness as the Lord desires? Then I asked: Are you producing the fruit of righteousness? What do you and I need to do to be more obedient to the Lord? I can't answer these questions for you. Only you can. Perhaps this is a good time for you to ask these questions of yourself. This may not feel good at the time of your correction, but the fruit produced will be well worth your efforts.

> *Now no chastening seems to be joyful for the present, but painful; nevertheless, afterward it yields the peaceable fruit of righteousness to those who have been trained by it.* (Hebrews 12:11)

If you receive the chastening of the Lord as you answer these questions, remember that it is a good thing. The chastening may be unpleasant, but it produces fruit. In this case, it produces the very thing we are concerned about. It produces *"the peaceable fruit of righteousness."* Don't resist the Lord. He is doing it all for your benefit. I know He is doing it for my benefit.

> *But the wisdom that is from above is first pure, then peaceable, gentle, willing to yield, full of mercy and good fruits, without partiality and without hypocrisy. Now the fruit of righteousness is sown in peace by those who make peace.* (James 3:17-18)

4. FRUIT OF YOUR LIPS

Therefore by Him let us continually offer the sacrifice of praise to God, that is, the fruit of our lips, giving thanks to His name. (Hebrews 13:15)

The writer of the book of Hebrews gives us some simple but profound ways to produce the right kind of fruit with our lips. It is no surprise that these are the behaviors that produce the righteous things the Lord is seeking from our service. Praise is a powerful fruit in the spiritual realm. Praise opens doors, releases the Lord's protection, establishes His Shalom, opens the floodgates of Heaven, and defeats the work of the enemy. Jehoshaphat had the praise team lead the warriors into the battle. When they arrived the Lord had already defeated the enemy forces for them. The Lord used their praise to open the doors of victory.

Giving thanks is another powerful weapon of spiritual warfare. I once made a study of how the Lord reacts to people who grumble, complain, and rebel against Him. The end was not good for any of them. So I made a study of how thanksgiving and praise are received by the Lord. He always blesses, multiplies, and protects those who are continuously giving Him words of gratitude. This may be a good time to do some spiritual introspection. Are you more likely to grumble and complain or to give Him thanks for everything?

Abide in Me, and I in you. As the branch cannot bear fruit of itself, unless it abides in the vine, neither can you, unless you abide in Me. (John 15:4)

If you need a little help with your attitude and actions toward the Lord, I have some good news. It is the Lord who is doing the work through you. In Isaiah 57:19 He says, "*I create the fruit of the lips: Peace, peace to him who is far off and to him who is near,*" *says the Lord,* "*and I will heal him.*" The fruit of the lips produces more than what we give to the Lord. He gives back more than we can ever release to Him. In the next two passages, consider what the good fruit of our lips does for us.

A man will be satisfied with good by the fruit of his mouth, and the recompense of a man's hands will be rendered to him. (Proverbs 12:14)

A man's stomach shall be satisfied from the fruit of his mouth; from the produce of his lips he shall be filled. (Proverbs 18:20)

5. FRUIT OF THE WOMB

Elizabeth was filled with the Holy Spirit. Then she spoke out with a loud voice and said, "Blessed are you among women, and blessed is the fruit of your womb! (Luke 1:41b-42)

When you read the passage above there is a temptation to limit this to the life and work of Yeshua. It is that, but I believe the Lord intends more for you and me. Remember how Yeshua said, "*Most assuredly, I say to you, he who believes in Me, the works that I do he will do also; and greater works than these he will do, because I go to My Father*" (John 14:12). I believe this also speaks about you as a blessed fruit of the Lord. Even when you were in your mother's womb, this was true for both Him and you.

Remember the words of David in Psalm 22:10, "*I was cast upon You from birth. From My mother's womb You have been My God.*" The words of the Lord given to Jeremiah are also for us. The Lord is releasing the same message to you and me, "*Before I formed you in the womb I knew you; before you were born I sanctified you; I ordained you a prophet to the nations.*" (Jeremiah 1:5) Think about it. You too were the blessed fruit in your mother's womb. Meditate on it as you read the passage below aloud.

> *Behold, children are a heritage from the Lord, the fruit of the womb is a reward.* (Psalm 127:3)

PROTECTION AGAINST REPROACH

> *I will multiply the yield of fruit from the trees and increase production in the fields, so that you never again suffer the reproach of famine among the nations.* (Ezekiel 36:30, CJB)

I wanted you to think again about the promise given to us by the Lord through the prophet Ezekiel. Look now at that last part: "*never again suffer the reproach of famine among the nations.*" This is a sudden, yet powerful shift in what the Lord is promising. When we fail to obey the Lord, the blessings of the Lord are no longer visible in our lives and work. This gives a bad witness to the nations. The normal response is for the nations to begin to reproach us for our hardships. This also brings reproach on the Lord's name. We must always work to protect the name of the Lord. We must live in a way that will bring honor and glory to the Lord. Amen?

> *The Lord will answer and say to His people, "Behold, I will send you grain and new wine and oil, and you will be satisfied by them; I will no longer make you a reproach among the nations.* (Joel 2:19)

As people see the blessing and favor of the Lord in your life and ministry, it brings honor and glory to His name. The Lord is always good to us and promises to take care of us even when we have failed Him. If we repent and return, He will open the floodgates of heaven and pour out more than we can contain. If you need to repent and return, don't hesitate. Repentance doesn't bring the reproach, it releases you from it. Even in times when those of the world reproach you, remember the promises of the Lord in the two passages below.

> *This is a faithful saying and worthy of all acceptance. For to this end we both labor and suffer reproach, because we trust in the living God, who is the Savior*

of all men, especially of those who believe. These things command and teach. (1 Timothy 4:9-11)

Listen to Me, you who know righteousness, you people in whose heart is My law: Do not fear the reproach of men, nor be afraid of their insults. For the moth will eat them up like a garment, and the worm will eat them like wool; but My righteousness will be forever, and My salvation from generation to generation." (Isaiah 51:7-8)

MINISTRY TIME

When we do meetings and teach these things, we usually end the sessions with a time of ministry to individuals. We desire to release the promises of the Lord to people and pray for them to receive and activate each one. One of the things we began to do several years ago was to give an impartation for increase and to release the promise of multiplication to the Lord's people. During one particular season, the Lord asked us to release a six-fold blessing. This was based on what the Lord did for Obed-Edom during the kingship of David.

So David would not move the ark of the LORD with him into the City of David; but David took it aside into the house of Obed-Edom the Gittite. The ark of the Lord remained in the house of Obed-Edom the Gittite three months. And the Lord blessed Obed-Edom and all his household. (2 Samuel 6:10-11)

As I studied that passage, I pondered a question in my mind: How did the Lord bless Obed-Edom so much that it impressed David to return to his plan of bringing the Ark of the Covenant to Jerusalem? Most English Bibles do not explain this. As I studied the Tanach, I was referred to the Talmud. This whole thing has been kept clear in Jewish history. In most Biblical footnotes it is said that Obed-Edom who kept the ark was not a Hebrew because He is called a "Gittite." This was usually said to identify someone from Gath like Goliath the Gittite. But Gath had originally been a Levitical city where the tribe of Kohath resided. By the way, they were gatekeepers. Many people including some Jews from Gath returned with David to Israel. The Talmud says that Obed-Edom was one of them and he later became a gatekeeper in the Temple.

I hope you were able to follow this. I led you through it to understand how Obed-Edom was blessed so much in three months that David gained courage from his blessing. We know from scripture that Obed-Edom had eight sons. However, in First Chronicles chapter sixteen, we are told that suddenly there were sixty-eight males in his household. According to the Talmud, Obed-Edom's wife and eight daughters-in-law all gave birth to six male children during those three months. The Talmud compares this to the multiplication of male children in Egypt which brought fear to Pharaoh and the people.

However you may choose to interpret this, the Lord told me to release the six-fold blessing of Obed-Edom and his family to the people in the meetings. Some people were skeptical as you may have guessed. Some drew back because they didn't want to give birth to six children. The Lord's promise was not about children when it was released in our meetings. I was not told to convince them, but offer the blessing to anyone who would receive it. In a one-on-one session with a pastor and his family, I released this again and He said he felt a shift in His faith. As he left the room, he checked his bank account and was amazed to see that he had exactly six times as much money in the bank. He had been praying for help to move to a new place of ministry and this increase made it possible for him. Another pastor received a six-fold increase of less dramatic proportions.

I know some people have trouble accepting these things. I have received many rebukes from people for teaching this, but I choose to obey the Lord even if some people are offended. Each of us needs to do a faith check from time to time. How is your faith? As we minister in the meetings, we often pray for people to receive increase and multiplication. Some do and some don't receive it. Why? I believe Yeshua answered this question in Matthew 8:13, "*Then Jesus said to the centurion, "Go your way; and as you have believed, so let it be done for you."* Those who believe for more will receive more. Amen? I want to release this to you as we do in our meetings. I provided a passage for you in the next section to help you receive this impartation from the Lord. Believe, receive, and activate them for yourself.

IMPARTATION FOR INCREASE AND MULTIPLICATION

Return to the stronghold, you prisoners of hope. Even today I declare that I will restore double to you. For I have bent Judah, My bow, fitted the bow with Ephraim, and raised up your sons, O Zion, against your sons, O Greece, and made you like the sword of a mighty man." Then the LORD will be seen over them, and His arrow will go forth like lightning. The Lord GOD will blow the trumpet, and go with whirl-winds from the south. The LORD of hosts will defend them; they shall devour and subdue with slingstones. They shall drink and roar as if with wine; they shall be filled with blood like basins, like the corners of the altar. The LORD their God will save them in that day, as the flock of His people. For they shall be like the jewels of a crown, lifted like a banner over His land— (Zechariah 9:12-16)

ACTIVATION

I have provided a few passages of scripture for your use in activating the promises of God. Read each aloud several times until they anchor in your heart. Then take some time to speak aloud your willingness to receive the promises of the Lord. Base everything on the Word of God. Believe it, receive it, and activated it with the faith the Lord has put in your heart. Look back over your life and remember all the ways the

Lord has kept His promises. Also, reflect on the times when He has multiplied His blessings for you.

Return to the stronghold, you prisoners of hope. Even today I declare that I will restore double to you. (Zechariah 9:12)

But you shall be named the priests of the Lord, they shall call you the servants of our God. You shall eat the riches of the Gentiles, and in their glory you shall boast. Instead of your shame you shall have double honor, and instead of confusion they shall rejoice in their portion. Therefore in their land they shall possess double; everlasting joy shall be theirs. "For I, the Lord, love justice; I hate robbery for burnt offering; I will direct their work in truth, and will make with them an everlasting covenant. Their descendants shall be known among the Gentiles, and their offspring among the people. All who see them shall acknowledge them, that they are the posterity whom the Lord has blessed." (Isaiah 61:6-9)

Instead of your shame you shall have double honor, and instead of confusion they shall rejoice in their portion. Therefore in their land they shall possess double; everlasting joy shall be theirs. (Isaiah 61:7)

FINAL NOTE

For a good tree does not bear bad fruit, nor does a bad tree bear good fruit. For every tree is known by its own fruit. For men do not gather figs from thorns, nor do they gather grapes from a bramble bush. A good man out of the good treasure of his heart brings forth good; and an evil man out of the evil treasure of his heart brings forth evil. For out of the abundance of the heart his mouth speaks. (Luke 6:43-45)

SELAH QUESTIONS

(Selah means to pause and meditate on these things.)

1. Explain the Lord's preferred type of math for His children.

_____

_____

_____

2. How do you see the Lord's multiplication in Shabbat?

_____

_____

_____

3. Explain how the Lord's multiplication increases with each appointed time?

_____

_____

_____

4. List the various types of fruit referenced in the Word of God.

_____

_____

_____

5. How does the Lord protect us from reproach?

_____

_____

_____

6. How does the Lord at times use reproach to bless us?

_____

_____

_____

7. In what ways have you experienced the Lord's multiplication in your life?

_____

_____

_____

GLOSSARY OF HEBREW WORDS AND NAMES

Moadim	Appointed Times – including Shabbat
Moed in space	Place of meeting
Moed in time	A point in time for meeting
Ohel Moed	Tent of Meeting
Shabbat	The seventh day of rest
manna	Bread from heaven
Shmita or Shemittah	A Sabbath rest for the land every seven years
Yovel (Jubilee)	Every 50 years, release and freedom are given for the land and people
Omer	Counting days (Pesach to Shavuot – Pentecost) Also a dry weight of approximately two quarts
TANACH	Hebrew scriptures which include both the Torah and all the other writings we call the Old Testament

| Talmud | A great collection of Jewish wisdom and history |

CHAPTER NINE

I Have Spoken and I Will Do It

I the Lord have spoken, and I will do it. (Ezekiel 17:24b, NIV)

The word of the Lord never returns void after He has spoken it. Do you believe this? Many people say they believe that the Word of the Lord never fails, but their behavior tells a different story. Some people speak more about their doubts than they speak about their faith. At times they seem to attribute more power and influence to the devil than to the Lord. Consider what the Lord said in Isaiah 55:11, KJV: "*So shall My word be that goes forth from My mouth; it shall not return to Me void, but it shall accomplish what I please, and it shall prosper in the thing for which I sent it.*" I like the last part of this passage from Isaiah. His word shall prosper in whatever the Lord has sent it to accomplish.

The Lord has been telling us that we can trust His word since the beginning of time, but we have been slow to learn. In each generation, His people have to be reminded again and again. Think about what the Lord spoke to Jacob in the passage below. Then apply it to you, your family, and your ministry. He will not depart from you until all He has spoken over you has been completed. He does not start something and then abandon those He has sent to accomplish His Word. The big question here is: Do you trust Him? Do you believe His Word?

> *Behold, I am with you and will keep you wherever you go, and will bring you back to this land; for I will not leave you until I have done what I have spoken to you.* (Genesis 28:15)

Past generations have testified that through all the good times and the bad, the Lord has kept every promise He has made. Has this been true in your life and your relationship with the Lord? Sometimes it is good to reflect on the ways the Lord has kept his promises in your life. This is one of the great strengths of David and maybe one of the reasons why He is referred to as a man after God's own heart. Most of the Psalms are written in the same way. Notice how the psalmist credits the Lord with everything that happens on the earth.

> *The Lord takes pleasure in those who fear Him, in those who hope in His mercy. Praise the Lord, O Jerusalem! Praise your God, O Zion! For He has strengthened the bars of your gates; He has blessed your children within you. He makes peace in your borders, and fills you with the finest wheat. He sends out His command to the earth; His word runs very*

swiftly. He gives snow like wool; He scatters the frost like ashes; He casts out His hail like morsels; who can stand before His cold? He sends out His word and melts them; He causes His wind to blow, and the waters flow. (Psalm 147:11-18)

After more than fifty years in the Lord's service, Joshua said, *"Not one of all the Lord's good promises to the house of Israel failed; every one was fulfilled."* (Joshua 21:45, NIV) This is an amazing and wonderful testimony about trusting the Lord as the greatest promise keeper of all time. You can always trust Him. He will do what He says He will do. He will keep all His promises given to past generations and you. The Lord is consistent throughout all of human history. What He has done in the past, He will do for you in your generation. Amen? Remember the praise given by David in the Psalm below. Perhaps it is a good time to bless the Lord with all your soul and spirit. Amen?

Bless the Lord, O my soul; and all that is within me, bless His holy name! Bless the Lord, O my soul, and forget not all His benefits: Who forgives all your iniquities, Who heals all your diseases, Who redeems your life from destruction, Who crowns you with lovingkindness and tender mercies, Who satisfies your mouth with good things, so that your youth is renewed like the eagle's. (Psalm 103:1-5)

BELIEVE HIS PROMISES

I have often noticed that people say they believe that the Lord kept His promise in days of old, and yet they doubt that the Lord will do it for them. This is not trust and it is certainly not based on faith. It is essential for us to believe the promises to receive them. We must believe they are for us to activate them. Without this faith, the Bible is just a storybook filled with legends that have no relevance for us. I don't know about you, but this is not what I believe about the Bible. To me, it is just as real and just as powerful today as it was on the day it was written. The promises are as real for me as they were for those who first heard them. Amen?

> Thus says the Lord God: *"On the day that I cleanse you from all your iniquities, **I will** also enable you to dwell in the cities, and the ruins shall be rebuilt. The desolate land shall be tilled instead of lying desolate in the sight of all who pass by. So they will say, 'This land that was desolate has become like the garden of Eden; and the wasted, desolate, and ruined cities are now fortified and inhabited.' Then the nations which are left all around you shall know that I, the Lord, have rebuilt the ruined places and planted what was desolate. **I, the Lord, have spoken it, and I will do it."*** (Ezekiel 36:33-36)

As you can see from this passage, the issue here is trust. Do you trust the Lord to fulfill all His promises? Don't give a casual answer to this question. Think about it. Peter was certain that he would never deny and betray the Lord, but before the day was over he had done it three times. All of the disciples (minus Judas) swore they would never leave Him, but all of them departed that same night. It is simple and easy to swear allegiance in the Upper Room, but very difficult in the garden of trials or the courtrooms of unjust human legalism.

The disciples discovered the hard way that they didn't know the depth of their courage or loyalty. These were blind spots in their self-awareness. Before we judge them, we need to take a close and honest look into our character defects. We all have blind spots in our spiritual being and we need help to see them. Once again ask the Spirit of truth to come and fulfill one of the powerful promises of Yeshua. *"However, when He, the Spirit of truth, has come, He will guide you into all truth; for He will not speak on His own authority, but whatever He hears He will speak; and He will tell you things to come."* (John 16:13) Place a claim on the promise that He will guide you into all truth. Ask Him to reveal all the truth you can handle at this time, and then to release more as you become strong enough to handle it.

The Lord declares: "I will do it!" The Lord has made this proclamation and given this powerful promise more than once. Earlier He had spoken through Ezekiel. He asked the people this same question. Will you stay strong, endure, and be courageous by trusting Me? These words are my summary of this section. Here is the exact quote from the Lord: *"Will your courage endure or your hands be strong in the day I deal with you? I the Lord have spoken, and I will do it.* (Ezekiel 22:14,

NIV) In every generation, the Lord's people must make their own decision about trusting Him and His promises. Now it is our turn and the challenge has come down to you and me. Who will you trust? Will you follow the wisdom of the world or the voice of the Holy Spirit? Will you hear the truth and believe this: when the Lord makes a promise, He will keep that promise? He does not waver back and forth. He is trustworthy all day every day for eternity.

> *Therefore say unto them, Thus saith the Lord God; There shall none of my words be prolonged any more, but the word which I have spoken shall be done, saith the Lord God.* (Ezekiel 12:28, KJV)

WHY DOES HE COMMIT TO THIS?

Over and over from one generation to the next, people have let the Lord down. They speak with their mouths, but the truth is seen in their behavior. In Matthew 15:8-9, Yeshua speaks the truth: "*These people draw near to Me with their mouth, and honor Me with their lips, but their heart is far from Me. and in vain they worship Me, teaching as doctrines the commandments of men.*" So why does the Lord reach out to every generation with promises He will keep despite the behavior of His followers? This is the question that kept coming to me as I worked through all these promises. Listen carefully to what He spoke through Isaiah the prophet:

For My own sake, for My own sake, I will do it; for how should My name be profaned? And I will not give My glory to another. Listen to Me, O Jacob, and Israel, My called: I am He, I am the First, I am also the Last. (Isaiah 48:11-12)

A profound sadness came over me as I read the passage above. I began to do some deep introspection. How many times have I let the Lord down while He was faithfully keeping all His promises to me? I went through several days of spending time repenting for my behavior and that of other believers. I remembered how Daniel confessed for the whole nation and I felt encouraged to do the same for His people in this generation. Daniel was a righteous man, but as a citizen, he felt the responsibility for what the nation had done.

Then I set my face toward the Lord God to make request by prayer and supplications, with fasting, sackcloth, and ashes. And I prayed to the Lord my God, and made confession, and said, "O Lord, great and awesome God, who keeps His covenant and mercy with those who love Him, and with those who keep His commandments, we have sinned and committed iniquity, we have done wickedly and rebelled, even by departing from Your precepts and Your judgments. Neither have we heeded your servants the prophets, who spoke in Your name to our kings and our princes, to our fathers and all the people of the land. O Lord, righteousness belongs to You, but to us shame of face, as it is this day—to the men of Judah, to the inhabitants of Jerusalem and all Israel, those near and those far off in all the countries to which You have driven them, because of the unfaithfulness which they have committed against You. (Daniel 9:3-7)

As a citizen of a nation, we are to some degree held accountable for what this nation has done and is doing. Perhaps we need to pray Daniel's prayer of repentance in the passage above. And after we have done this, we can go to that chapter in the book of Daniel and pray more of His prayers which touched the heart of God. The fact is that there are times when the Lord has been abused by His people. At times the sins of the people have gone beyond His grace and tolerance as well as His high level of mercy and longsuffering. Think about this as you study the passage below. We need some modern-day Daniels to be on their knees in repentance. We don't want to go as far away from the Lord as the people did in Isaiah's generation.

*I have held My peace a long time, I have been still and restrained Myself. Now **I will** cry like a woman in labor, **I will** pant and gasp at once. **I will** lay waste the mountains and hills, and dry up all their vegetation; **I will** make the rivers coastlands, and **I will** dry up the pools. **I will** bring the blind by a way they did not know; **I will** lead them in paths they have not known. **I will** make darkness light before them, and crooked places straight. These things **I will** do for them, and not forsake them.* (Isaiah 42:14-16)

As I repented, I prayed over and over that the Lord's people in this generation have not gone too far. I pray that it is not too late. I am so encouraged by how the Lord ended the message given through Isaiah. The Lord quickly moves from judgment to restoration. We have an awesome Father God who always leads with mercy – thus His name Adonai (God of Mercy). The Lord does it for our good, but we must never forget that He also acts to keep His name holy. Remember what He said in Isaiah 48:11, *"For My own sake, for My own sake, I will do it; for how should My name be profaned? And I will not give My glory to another.*

PROMISES OF JUDGMENT ALSO KEPT

Remember that the Lord keeps all His promises. This means that He also keeps His promises of judgment. He is Adonai (God of mercy), but He is also Elohim (God of Justice). The Lord prefers mercy but will give judgment when there is no other way to get the attention of His people. Remember that He does what He says He will do. He restated these words in the prophecy of coming judgment. Remember what we said earlier. He is the ultimate promise keeper and He leaves the choice to us. What will we choose – mercy or judgment? It is not what our mouths say that counts. It is what we prove by our repentance and obedient behavior.

> *I, the Lord, have spoken it; it shall come to pass, and I will do it; I will not hold back, nor will I spare, nor will I relent; according to your ways and according*

to your deeds They will judge you, says the Lord God.
(Ezekiel 24:14)

What does the behavior of this generation say about our trust and obedience? As I wrote this part of the book, the old song, "Trust and Obey" came into my mind. It suddenly occurred to me that the previous generation may have dealt better with this issue than our supposedly wiser and more informed generation. Sometimes it is a good thing to go back to the time of our fathers and mothers to learn the lessons needed to live in a right relationship with the Lord in our time. Think about it as you read through the words of this song or better yet sing the words of this old hymn.

> *When we walk with the Lord in the light of His Word,*
> *What a glory He sheds on our way!*
> *While we do His good will, He abides with us still,*
> *And with all who will trust and obey.*
>
> *Refrain:*
> *Trust and obey, for there's no other way*
> *To be happy in Jesus, but to trust and obey.*
> (public domain)

I was encouraged greatly by what Yeshua said in the Gospel of John. Yeshua began to make some fresh new "I will" statements to his disciples and to everyone who would believe in Him. We often read the first part of this teaching without the later part. Yeshua gives two powerful "I will do" promises to believers. This will be done for you and me so that the Father may be glorified. Now I will say it another way. The Lord continues to give these amazing promises and then keeps them to give glory to the Father. For His name's sake, He will keep these promises for you. Amen?

Most assuredly, I say to you, he who believes in Me, the works that I do he will do also; and greater works than these he will do, because I go to My Father. And whatever you ask in My name, that I will do, that the Father may be glorified in the Son. If you ask anything in My name, I will do it. (John 14:12-14)

OUR TURN TO OBEY THE LORD

Now therefore, go, lead the people to the place of which I have spoken to you. Behold, My Angel shall go before you. (Exodus 32:34)

At times it becomes our task to help carry out the Lord's promises in the lives of others. Just as the Lord sent Moses to keep His word, He calls us to be carriers of the fulfillment of His promises. Think of it this way: at least He is not asking you to fulfill a promise for two million people. Think about it. It was as difficult for Moses as it is for you when the Lord sends you. Think about how difficult and fearful it was for Ananias to be the carrier of God's promise to a much-feared man called Saul of Tarsus.

Now there was a certain disciple at Damascus named Ananias; and to him the Lord said in a vision, "Ananias." And he said, "Here I am, Lord." So the Lord said to him, "Arise and go to the street called Straight, and inquire at the house of Judas for one called Saul of Tarsus, for behold, he is praying. And in a vision he has seen a man named Ananias coming in and putting his hand on him, so that he might receive his sight." Then Ananias answered, "Lord, I have heard from many about this man, how much harm he has done to Your saints in Jerusalem. And here he has authority from the chief priests to bind all who call on Your name." But the Lord said to him, "Go, for he is a chosen vessel of Mine to bear My name before Gentiles, kings, and the children of Israel. For I will show him how many things he must suffer for My name's sake." (Acts 9:10-19)

Though Ananias was filled with fear, he chose to obey the Lord. Think about this calling on Ananias' life as you reflect a little more on the passage above. Is the Lord calling you to take a life-changing word to someone today? Are you the instrument of His promise for another person right now? Don't let fear stop you. Don't disobey the Lord because the task seems great. Remember what the Lord spoke about you in the passage from John 14:12-14 in the section above. Remember that the Lord will be with you. You and the Lord are an awesome team, and you can do what He calls you to do. Amen?

PRAYER

Some of the passages I am sharing with you in this chapter are a little long, but all that is in each passage is important for you to help you accomplish your tasking from the Lord. One of the things I practice is to pray the prayers in the Bible given by the Lord's trusted leaders and apostles. Think about it. They are in God's Word. They have effected people in amazing ways in the past. They can release the same faith and spiritual authority to you as they did for the Lord's people of old. Even though the prayer below is long, it is filled with what we need most as we serve the Lord in our generation. Don't simply read these prayers, pray them as your prayers. Expect the Lord to release His answers for you. Remember how the Lord said to the Centurion, "Let it be unto you as you have believed."

His intent was that now, through the church, the manifold wisdom of God should be made known to the rulers and authorities in the heavenly realms, according to his eternal purpose which he accomplished in Christ Jesus our Lord. In him and through faith in him we may approach God with freedom and confidence. I ask you, therefore, not to be discouraged because of my sufferings for you, which are your glory. For this reason I kneel before the Father, from whom his whole family in heaven and on earth derives its name. I pray that out of his glorious riches he may strengthen you with power through his Spirit in your inner being, so that Christ may dwell in your hearts through faith. And I pray that you, being rooted and established in love, may have power, together with all the saints, to grasp how wide and long and high and deep is the love of Christ, and to know this love that surpasses knowledge—that you may be filled to the measure of all the fullness of God. Now to him who is able to do immeasurably more than all we ask or imagine, according to his power that is at work within us, to him be glory in the church and in Christ Jesus throughout all generations, for ever and ever! Amen. (Ephesians 3:10-21, NIV)

ACTIVATION

One of the most powerful ways we have to activate the Lord's promises in our lives is to lift up our praises to Him. This is another area of our relationship with the Lord where we can find help in His Word. Some of the greatest statements of praise are found in scripture especially in the Psalms. Choose one of the promises of God which you desire to manifest in your life and begin first to open your heart with praises to Him for what He has done for you in the past. After a time of praise, then place your demand on the promise and expect to receive what you ask. This method also blesses you to be prepared because these praises are great faith builders. Use the passage below to praise Father God and to build up your faith to receive great things from the Lord.

Praise Adonai, my soul! I will praise Adonai as long as I live. I will sing praise to my God all my life. Don't put your trust in princes, or mortals, who cannot help. When they breathe their last, they return to dust; on that very day all their plans are gone. Happy is he whose help is Ya'akov's God, whose hope is in Adonai his God. He made heaven and earth, the sea, and everything in them; he keeps faith forever. He secures justice for the oppressed, he gives food to the hungry. Adonai sets prisoners free. Adonai opens the eyes of the blind; Adonai lifts up those who are bent over. Adonai loves the righteous. Adonai watches over strangers, he sustains the fatherless and widow; but the way of the wicked he twists. (Psalm 146:1-9, CJB)

Don't forget to end this activation time with praise and thanksgiving for the things which the Lord is going to manifest in your life. Faith is not what you see, but what you expect to see. Remember the powerful teaching in Hebrews 11:1-3, "*Now faith is the substance of things hoped for, the evidence of things not seen. For by it the elders obtained a good testimony. By faith we understand that the worlds were framed by the word of God, so that the things which are seen were not made of things which are visible.*" The Lord brings things that are not into existence. He is faithful and is as powerful today as when His words were first spoken. Put you faith in Him and receive what He promises even before they become visible. Amen?

SELAH QUESTIONS

(Selah means to pause and meditate on these things.)

1. What assurance do you have that the Lord will keep His promises?

_____

_____

_____

2. What testimonies can you list about Him keeping His promises to you?

_____

_____

_____

3. Can you name the reason for His promises given in this chapter?

_____

_____

_____

4. How do you show the Lord that you trust and obey?

_____

_____

_____

5. What has led you to trust in Yeshua as you trust in the Father?

_____

_____

_____

6. Why should you repent in this season?

_____

_____

_____

7. In what ways has fear held you back in the past?

_____

_____

_____

8. What is the role of praise in activating the promises of God?

_____

_____

_____

CHAPTER TEN

They Will Know That
I Am The Lord

Thus says the Lord God: "I will also let the house of Israel inquire of Me to do this for them: I will increase their men like a flock. Like a flock offered as holy sacrifices, like the flock at Jerusalem on its feast days, so shall the ruined cities be filled with flocks of men. **Then they shall know that I am the Lord."** (Ezekiel 36:37-38)

As the Lord continued to talk about restoration, multiplication, and increase, He made a powerful comment which is often ignored. I believe this tends to occur because of the repetition with which the Lord makes this comment in the scriptures. We should not ignore repetition by the Lord. This is the way He lets us know that He is committed to doing what He says. The repeated use of this strong statement has been treated by most casual readers much like a period at the end of a sentence, but it must not be ignored. Look at it again. He said, "*Then they shall know that I am the Lord.*" I went back to the verses before the ones we are using for this study and found that He also began His conversation similarly. The Lord said:

> *And I will sanctify My great name, which has been profaned among the nations, which you have profaned in their midst; **and the nations shall know that I am the Lord**, says the Lord God, when I am hallowed in you before their eyes.* (Ezekiel 36:23)

A question came to my mind. Didn't the children of Israel already know that He was the Lord? He said it over and over. He demonstrated it as He defeated all their enemies. He sealed the deal by adding it to all His promises. Then it occurred to me that they did not know Him. This led me to another thought. Many people who identify themselves as believers today don't appear to know the Lord. When I taught the message of the thirteen attributes of the Lord revealed in Exodus 34:5-7, I didn't find anyone who claimed to be familiar with this powerful revelation of the Lord which had dramatically been given to Moses to teach us about who He truly is. Because of this, I am convinced that His foundational words and glorious promises need to be spoken again in this generation. As you study these promises, notice that from beginning to end, Father God makes it clear that we are expected to know and acknowledge that He is the Lord. He takes this message even further. In the passage above, the Lord makes it clear that He wants everyone from every nation to know who He is.

This is good news. Because it means that He wants us to know in the depth of our hearts that He is our God and we can trust Him. As you begin to notice how many times throughout the Bible the Lord has felt it necessary to say, "I am the Lord?" make it your practice each time to stop and ponder anew what the Father is saying to you. In the New King James Version of the Bible, it is recorded that the Lord made this statement 168 times. As I noticed the frequency of this proclamation I wondered again why the people did not know this fact. As I continued this study, I found that often His people had forgotten Him after only one or two generations. They had forgotten the stories about all the amazing signs and wonders He had performed for them and their ancestors. At times, they even picked up the idols of their defeated enemies and began to believe these were their gods. Why pick a known loser over the greatest winner of all time?

> *Therefore prophesy and say to them, 'Thus says the Lord God: "Behold, O My people, I will open your graves and cause you to come up from your graves, and bring you into the land of Israel. **Then you shall know that I am the Lord**, when I have opened your graves, O My people, and brought you up from your graves. I will put My Spirit in you, and you shall live, and I will place you in your own land. **Then you shall know that I, the Lord, have spoken it and performed it**," says the Lord.'* (Ezekiel 37:12-14)

This proclamation was primarily meant for the children of Israel. You will notice that it was spoken directly to them more than to any other nation. It is something He wanted the children of Israel to know without question. I believe this is why He said it so often. Yet He made it clear from the beginning that it was not exclusively for them. Through Israel, the Lord planned to reach out to the entire human race. Remember His promise to Abraham in Genesis 12:3, "*I will bless those who bless you, and I will curse him who curses you; and in you all the families of the earth shall be blessed.*" This was and is Israel's destiny. They are to bring all the families of the earth to the Lord. Each of us is a child of God and He wants all His children to come home. Let me make this clear, the signs and wonders the Lord worked in Egypt were also given so the Egyptian people would come to know Him. "*And the Egyptians shall know that I am the Lord, when I stretch out My hand on Egypt and bring out the children of Israel from among them.*" (Exodus 7:5)

WHY IS THIS SO IMPORTANT?

Here is my thought on this matter. If it's important to the Lord, it is important to me. I look at this as a promise and proclamation which was not for Israel alone. It is being spoken once again to you and me in our generation. The Lord often said something like, "*Then the nations shall know that I am the LORD, the Holy One in Israel.*" (Ezekiel 39:7b) But we need to understand that it didn't end there. This is the beginning of the release of the promise and not just a limited one-time fulfillment. The Lord made it clear from the beginning that His blessings for Israel were intended to bless everyone on planet earth who would believe His promises and obey Him. Consider His proclamation during the exodus, "*But as truly as I live, all the earth shall be filled with the glory of the Lord.*" (Numbers 14:21, KJV) Do you believe this? Think about it. It was written for you and me to assist us in understanding and to build us up in our faith in The Lord.

This is an awesome thought. I have often tried to visualize what it will look like when the Earth is filled with the "glory of the Lord." As I said above, I always go back to the Lord's promise given to Abraham, "*… and in you all the families of the earth shall be blessed.*" (Genesis 12:3b) Abraham received it for us and helped to pass it down through the generations. I continued my research and came to another conclusion about why the Lord spoke this so often. He wanted them to understand at that time and He still wants to make it clear to His people. I think this was clearly stated in Jeremiah 32:27, "*Behold, I am the LORD, the God of all flesh.*" He is your God and He is my God. Amen?

From the beginning of time, the Lord worked to reveal Himself to His creation. Early on He became a friend to Abraham and visited him often to build a relationship and to release a revelation of who He is. As we study the Bible more and more, we see that this is a progressive revelation. In the appendix to my book, "Seeing the Unseen Realm", I pointed to the thirteen attributes of the Lord given to Moses on Mount Sinai. You can check that out for more information. This was the greatest self-disclosure of the Lord until the coming of Yeshua ha Messiach. In Yeshua, we see more clearly who the

Father truly is. Consider this truth as you reflect on the passage below. Yeshua is telling us that He is the revelation of the Father.

> Philip said to Him, "Lord, show us the Father, and it is sufficient for us." Jesus said to him, "Have I been with you so long, and yet you have not known Me, Philip? He who has seen Me has seen the Father; so how can you say, 'Show us the Father'? Do you not believe that I am in the Father, and the Father in Me? The words that I speak to you I do not speak on My own authority; but the Father who dwells in Me does the works. Believe Me that I am in the Father and the Father in Me, or else believe Me for the sake of the works themselves." (John 14:8-11)

LOOKING TO THE LORD'S REVELATION DISCOVERING WHO HE IS

Working through the Lord's promises for restoration required me to read this section of the Bible over and over in a variety of different translations. As I was doing this, I noticed that the Lord said something very important in Ezekiel 36:22-23a, "*Therefore say to the house of Israel, 'Thus says the Lord God: "I do not do this for your sake, O house of Israel, but for My holy name's sake, which you have profaned among the nations wherever you went. And I will sanctify My great name, which has been profaned among the nations, which you have profaned in their midst; and the nations shall know that I am the Lord," says the Lord God,*" I particularly took note of the last part of this passage when Father God declared, "*I am the Lord.*" I knew this was true. It was not new information, but it was something that touched me at a much deeper level in my spirit.

Consider this: The Lord did all of this so that all the nations would know that He is the Lord. His people had profaned His name through their wicked behavior and the Lord wanted to clear His name. Rather than taking greater steps to punish them, He took this opportunity to do even more for them to clear His name. Then it hit me that He did it for us. He revealed more and more of His character then and He is still doing it now. The last words of this chapter give the same message. "*Then they shall know that I am the Lord.*" (Ezekiel 36:38b) It then occurred to me that this seems to be important to the Lord.

As I took note of this, I began a personal journey of discovery to find out exactly what the Lord was saying. I looked for the unique explanations of what this should mean for us. I am sharing my learnings with you here in hopes that it will help you receive the Lord's self-revelation for yourself. I hope you will go even further than I did as you seek to know the Lord better. I pray that He will give you greater revelation as you read this than He did for me as I was writing it. Now, let's go on a journey to discover more and more about the nature and character of our amazing Father God.

WHO IS THE LORD OUR GOD?

1. HE IS THE ONE WHO HEALS.

If you diligently heed the voice of the Lord your God and do what is right in His sight, give ear to His commandments and keep all His statutes, I will put none of the diseases on you which I have brought on the Egyptians. For I am the Lord who heals you. (Exodus 15:26)

Have you noticed how many times we are told in the scriptures that the Lord is our healer? Yeshua is the perfect living revelation of the Father. This is why I speak over and over the prophecy about Him in Isaiah 53:5, "*But He was wounded for our transgressions, He was bruised for our iniquities; the chastisement for our peace was upon Him, and by His stripes we are healed.*" If you need healing, look to Yeshua. He is the embodiment of the healing character of God. Begin to receive the promise for your healing by faith and activate it by speaking it over and over until it manifests.

Think about it. It is a key part of God's nature to heal. He is not withholding His grace and power from us. Trust Him and begin to confess and praise Him for your healing before it manifests. Then keep on praising and thanking Him until it does manifest. After it manifests, continue to praise Him because this is one of the best ways to fully anchor your healing. People tend to give up so quickly. Don't give up on your healing. Have you ever noticed that the promise in Isaiah

53 was completed when Yeshua endured that horrible beating before going to the cross? You were healed at that time. Let it finally manifest as you add your faith to the promise. Think about and claim the Lord's promise to King Hezekiah, "*Thus says the Lord, the God of David your father: "I have heard your prayer, I have seen your tears; surely I will heal you.* (2 Kings 20:5) Now consider this: surely He is the Lord who will also heal you. Amen? Trust Him. He has heard your prayers and He will heal you. Amen?

2. HE IS OUR PROVIDER.

> *At twilight you shall eat meat, and in the morning you shall be filled with bread. And you shall know that I am the Lord your God.* (Exodus 16:12b)

Consider this: The Lord is saying that we will know Him by His provision for us. Isn't that amazing and wonderful? Even when the children of Israel were grumbling and complaining, He still provided for them. Even though they rebelled against Him, He continued to provide for them. Think about what He is ready and willing to do for you. Think about all that He has been doing for you without your awareness. He is an awesome and loving Father God. He spoke a great "I will" promise to David for the children of Israel: "*I will abundantly bless her provision; I will satisfy her poor with bread.* (Palm 132:15) Have you taken the time to receive these two "I will" promises of provision for you and your family? The only thing holding up your supernatural provision may be that you have not yet activated it by faith.

The Lord wants us to understand this. He wanted everyone to understand His nature of love, grace, mercy, and Shalom. So, He sent Yeshua to teach and model these things for us. Yeshua ha Messiach completed this mission. This is why He could proclaim on the cross, "*It is finished!*" Paul wanted to clarify the will and purpose of the Lord by teaching the believers in Rome: "*For if, by the trespass of the one man, death reigned through that one man, how much more will those who receive God's abundant provision of grace and of the gift of righteousness reign in life through the one man, Jesus Christ.* (Romans 5:17, NIV) Think about it. He promises to be your provider. Remember, He keeps His promises. He has released your provision, grace, and the gift of righteousness. Believe it. Receive it. Then activate the promises given in God's self-revelation of Himself as your Provider.

3. HE IS OUR GOD WHO BRINGS US OUT OF BONDAGE.

I am the Lord your God, who brought you out of the land of Egypt, out of the house of bondage. (Exodus 20:2)

The Lord spoke these words over and over to His followers. Why? The people kept forgetting who He was and what He had done for them in the past. It is through the testimonies of the past that the Lord builds our faith to walk in the fulfillment of all His promises. Look closely at the teachings and truths in Revelation 19:10, "*And I fell at his feet to worship him. But he said to me, "See that you do not do that! I am your fellow servant, and of your brethren who have the testimony of Jesus. Worship God! For the testimony of Jesus is the spirit of prophecy.*" Our testimonies about Yeshua are prophetic words that release the power of the promises again and again for His people in every generation.

Remembering what the Lord did in the past will give you trust in what He promises to do for you and me now and in the future. Let the testimonies of Yeshua release a prophetic word for you about how much the Father loves you, how much He wants to bless you, and how much He wants to restore you now and forever. Amen? Each time you read a passage about Yeshua healing someone, accept it as a healing testimony for you. This is one of the reasons why we need to spend much time in the Word of God. We need to hear the testimonies of the Father, the Son, and the Holy Spirit over and over to build up our faith so we will be able to receive these awesome promises.

4. HE IS THE LORD WHO SANCTIFIES YOU.

> *Speak also to the children of Israel, saying: Surely My Sabbaths you shall keep, for it is a sign between Me and you throughout your generations, that you may know that I am the Lord who sanctifies you.* (Exodus 31:13)

You don't hear much preaching or teaching about sanctification these days, but it is a major teaching in the Bible. I believe that one reason for the neglect is that people do not understand what this word means. For me, the best definition of sanctification is being set apart for the Lord and for the ministry He has given you. Whether we think much about it or not, the Lord is still setting people apart for His service. I believe it is better to understand and embrace it than to ignore it because some people do not want to hear it. I choose to obey the Lord rather than to submit to the desires of the world. How about you?

> *Consecrate yourselves therefore, and be holy, for I am the Lord your God. And you shall keep My statutes, and perform them: I am the Lord who sanctifies you.* (Leviticus 20:7-8)

As people read the message above from Leviticus, they may feel inadequate to do what is being required by the Lord. He says that we are to consecrate ourselves. How can we do that? To help you understand this better, you need to be clear that the meaning of this word has been twisted over time. The twisted version of this word has pushed many people away from understanding what the Lord is expecting of us. Consecration as described by the Lord is about taking physical steps to clean up and remain clean before the Lord. When the Lord told Israel to consecrate them, they were expected to take a bath and put on clean clothes. Then they were to avoid touching things which would make them ceremonially unclean. Think about this as you read the passage below. When the Lord told the people to leave the places where they had been captive and return to Zion, He said,

*Depart! Depart! Go out from there, **touch no unclean thing;** Go out from the midst of her, **be clean**, you who bear the vessels of the Lord. For you shall not go out with haste, nor go by flight; for the Lord will go before you, and the God of Israel will be your rear guard.* (Isaiah 52:11-12)

We clean ourselves physically so the Lord can cleanse us spiritually. The word "holy" in the Bible is another word for being set apart for the Lord and living in a way that will demonstrate our commitment to Him. After we have been delivered from bondage, the Lord asks us to know and obey His statutes. Then comes the good news. The Lord will sanctify us spiritually. He does for us what we cannot do for ourselves. It is like a partnership with the Lord. We do the things we are capable of doing and He does the things which are impossible for us. Wow! What an awesome God!

5. HE IS THE LORD WHO MAKES YOU HOLY.

For I am the Lord who brings you up out of the land of Egypt, to be your God. You shall therefore be holy, for I am holy. (Leviticus 11:45)

I have frequently been told by people that they cannot be holy. This is something that seems too high and too lofty for them. How quickly we forget that it is the Lord who does this work. It is by faith in Yeshua that these spiritual things are accredited to us. He did the work and we just need to believe in Him, love Him, and obey what He has told us to do. He says,

"*Be Holy!*" However, you need to remember that He prefaced this by saying, "*For I am the Lord your God. You shall therefore consecrate yourselves, and you shall be holy; for I am holy. Neither shall you defile yourselves with any creeping thing that creeps on the earth.*" (Leviticus 11:44)

We consecrate ourselves (get physically clean) and the Lord does the rest. He is looking for people who are willing to follow Him. He desires people who seek Him with a holy hunger to be in a loving relationship with Him. He does not ask for more than we can give. He does not ask us to do things that we are incapable of doing. He gives us what we need to offer back to Him. Be Holy! In other words, set your heart aside to love Him and give your service to Him. Now equipped with this information study and understand what the Lord is saying to you in the passage below:

> *Blessed be the God and Father of our Lord Jesus Christ, who has blessed us with every spiritual blessing in the heavenly places in Christ, just as He chose us in Him before the foundation of the world, that we should be holy and without blame before Him in love, having predestined us to adoption as sons by Jesus Christ to Himself, according to the good pleasure of His will, to the praise of the glory of His grace, by which He made us accepted in the Beloved.* (Ephesians 1:3-6)

6. HE IS YOUR ONE AND ONLY SAVIOR.

I, even I, am the Lord, and besides Me there is no savior. I have declared and saved, I have proclaimed, and there was no foreign god among you; Therefore you are My witnesses," says the Lord, "that I am God. Indeed before the day was, I am He; and there is no one who can deliver out of My hand; I work, and who will reverse it?" (Isaiah 43:11-13)

It always amazes me that people who proclaim that they are progressive and know more than previous generations of the Lord still abandon Him and go after gods who are not real. It is happening again in our generation. People are seeing themselves as more holy and wise than the Lord. They judge and criticize Him for things they do not understand. This hasn't worked well for previous generations and it will not work well in this one either. There is only one God. Remember what the Lord said in Isaiah 45:5a, *"I am the Lord, and there is no other; there is no God besides Me."* The Lord spoke these words over and over to countless generations. Now He is speaking them to us.

No matter how politically correct it may seem for people to embrace other religions, this is a false teaching. When we cave in to the pressure of political correctness, we are enabling people to lead lives that will be judged by the Lord. There is only one savior. No other god can deliver you from the hand of the Lord. With all the revelation He has given there is no excuse for being unaware of Who He is. Yeshua is still the way, the truth, and the life. It is still true that there is no other way to the Father except through Him. Amen?

> *I am the Lord, and there is no other; there is no God besides Me. I will gird you, though you have not known Me, that they may know from the rising of the sun to its setting that there is none besides Me. I am the Lord, and there is no other; I form the light and create darkness, I make peace and create calamity; I, the Lord, do all these things.* (Isaiah 45:5-7)

Our Father God looked around and saw that there was no other god. Did He do this to reassure Himself? Of course not. He always knew this. He was taking His people through a process of building their faith. Think about it. If the Lord cannot find another god, who can? He created all things. He sustains and maintains everything in the Universe. When other people challenge you to accept and approve of other belief systems, keep your faith strong in the Word of God. The key is to trust what the Lord said in Isaiah 45:5-7. There is no other God. Once again I declare that I would rather be true to God and be judged by people than to follow people and be judged by God. How about you? Do you stand with the Lord or with the crowd?

7. HE IS THE CREATOR AND REDEEMER.

> *I am the Lord, your Holy One, the Creator of Israel, your King."* (Isaiah 43:15)

When people who follow worldly wisdom listen to the fear-based news media they are constantly living in fear that the world is falling apart. These programs troll for listeners by deceiving people into believing that the planet is being destroyed by reckless people. People are often told that they must take action to redeem our planet. Unfortunately, their advice about what to do is seriously flawed. I am in favor of being responsible for the protection of our environment. It is good stewardship to do this, but it is a false hope to think that with our intellect and labor we can make the earth, our solar system, and the Universe work better.

One volcanic eruption can wipe out all the savings of greenhouse emissions during the past several years. Remember also that several volcanoes erupt every year in various parts of the earth. Other nations who demand that we be more responsible by giving them money, are not doing their share to keep the air clean and the earth productive. Human endeavor is powerless to do what false teachers claim we must do. Here is some plain truth: we need the Lord's help to keep the earth clean and productive. He is the creator and He is also the sustainer of our planet. He changes seasons, temperatures, winds, and rain to make the adjustments that only He can understand. Trust in the Lord. One day the earth will be replaced by a better one, but it will be a work of the Lord and not of humanity.

Thus says the Lord, your Redeemer, and He who formed you from the womb: "I am the Lord, who makes all things, Who stretches out the heavens

all alone, Who spreads abroad the earth by Myself;
(Isaiah 44:24)

After reading this chapter, my wife, Gloria, reminded me about an amazing heavenly vision the Lord had given to me. This experience assisted me in understanding a profound revelation about who He is as the creator. Before I was carried to Heaven in the vision, I had been reflecting on what Yeshua said in John 14:12, "*Most assuredly, I say to you, he who believes in Me, the works that I do he will do also; and greater works than these he will do, because I go to My Father.*" In the Throne Room of Heaven, I spoke out saying, "I want to be able to do what you do!" The Lord rose from His throne and told me to follow Him. We walked together through a long corridor which opened up to a room that only had three walls. Where the fourth wall would normally have been, I saw a huge opening which gave us a magnificent view of the Universe. It was awesome.

Then the Lord told me to watch carefully. He began to create a new star. It appeared to me that a long sheet made up of millions of photons of light was being rolled up over and over around the core of the little star. As I watched the star grew more and more. I asked the Lord about the wrapping of light. He told me that all the little photons contained His instructions. When complete the star would be programmed for its entire life cycle from its beginning until it exploded and became a supernova. The Lord looked at me and said, "That is what I do. Can you do that?" That was one humbling moment and I confessed that I could not do that.

I share this with you because of what I learned from this experience. No matter who we are or how well we are educated, we cannot create or maintain one single star or one single planet. We can only look to the true creator and seek His wisdom about how we are to live responsibly with what we have been given on this planet. Our greatest achievements can never fix or sustain the world or the Universe in which it resides. Our real task is to stay close to the creator and sustainer of the world in faith and assurance that He can and will do what is already in His plan. Some day He will create a new heaven and a new earth in which all things have been made perfect. Until then we live responsibly and in obedience to our Lord. Amen?

ACTIVATION PRAYER

O Lord, there is none like You, nor is there any God besides You, according to all that we have heard with our ears. And who is like Your people Israel, the one nation on the earth whom God went to redeem for Himself as a people—to make for Yourself a name by great and awesome deeds, by driving out nations from before Your people whom You redeemed from Egypt? For You have made Your people Israel Your very own people forever; and You, Lord, have become their God. And now, O Lord, the word which You have spoken concerning Your servant and concerning his house, let it be established forever, and do as You have said. So let it be established, that Your name may be magnified forever, saying, The Lord of hosts, the God of Israel, is Israel's God. And let the house of Your servant David be established before You. For You, O my God, have revealed to Your servant that You will build him a house. Therefore Your servant has found it in his heart to pray before You. And now, Lord, You are God, and have promised this goodness to Your servant. Now You have been pleased to bless the house of Your servant, that it may continue before You forever; for You have blessed it, O Lord, and it shall be blessed forever. (1 Chronicles 17:20-27)

SELAH QUESTIONS

(Selah means to pause and meditate on these things.)

1. Why does the Lord need to tell us over and over that He is the Lord?

_____

_____

_____

2. Why is it important for you to understand who He is and what He does?

_____

_____

_____

3. What is the Lord saying to you about who He is?

_____

_____

_____

4. Name three or more of the Lord's self-revelations associated with the "I am the Lord" statements.

_____

_____

_____

5. What part or parts of this study will you be able to apply in your own life and ministry?

_____

_____

_____

6. In what ways does the Lord move to sustain our planet?

_____

_____

_____

CHAPTER ELEVEN

For My Holy Name's Sake

Help us, O God of our salvation, for the glory of Your name; and deliver us, and provide atonement for our sins, for Your name's sake! (Psalm 79:9)

I want to examine in more depth and greater detail what I briefly discussed in Chapter Nine. The Lord made it clear that He often acts simply for His own name's sake. The Bible makes it clear that in some of His moves of restoration and judgment He is primarily acting to protect His name and reputation. Think about this: At times the actions by those who claim to be His people are an embarrassment for Him and the Kingdom of God. The only gospel some people will ever see is you – a living example of Who God is in the lives of people. When people see you living in humility and obedience, the Lord is built up and glorified. Think about it and then ask yourself some challenging questions. When people look at you is the Lord glorified or is His name tarnished by your behavior? It is a tough question, but one that each of us needs to answer in our own lives in His service. How do you characterize your own life? Are you a blessing or an embarrassment to the Lord?

Now consider this. When we look again at the "I will" promises of God, notice that something has been added to the basic formula for receiving, activating and releasing the promises of God in our lives and ministries. A new reason has been given for why the Lord releases these amazing and wonderful promises for people such as you and me. Look at it this way: when we properly receive His promises, activate them, and begin to live by them, we bring honor and glory to the Name of the Lord. When we fail to receive, activate, and/or live by His promises, we bring dishonor to His glorious Name. What is the outcome for the Lord's name in your life and mine? In the passage below, the Lord explains this very clearly for us through the prophet, Ezekiel.

> *Therefore say to the house of Israel, Thus says the Lord God: "I do not do this for your sake, O house of Israel, but for **My holy name's sake**, which **you have profaned** among the nations wherever you went. And **I will sanctify My great name**, which has been profaned among the nations, which you have profaned in their midst; and **the nations shall know that I am the Lord**," says the Lord God, "when I am hallowed in you before their eyes. For I will take you from among the nations, gather you out of all countries, and bring you into your own land.* (Ezekiel 36:22-24)

AT WHAT COST?

Some people may consider these things and then ask what it is going to cost on their part. There is something like spiritual laziness working amongst many of us. We like the benefits, but we are not certain if the cost/benefit ratio is large enough to prompt action. When people are considering this, they often miss how much the Lord has already done to make the restoration happen in their lives. Many people do not naturally consider how far He has already gone and or how great is the price He has already paid to bring these precious gifts to us. Many do not consider the great cost Yeshua has already paid to cancel our debt for us to be enabled to receive His reward. There is no comparison between the great and mighty things He has done and the meager requirements He has for us.

> *For My name's sake I will defer My anger, and for My praise I will restrain it from you, so that I do not cut you off. Behold, I have refined you, but not as silver; I have tested you in the furnace of affliction. For My own sake, for My own sake, I will do it; for how should My name be profaned? And I will not give My glory to another.* (Isaiah 48:9-11)

In the Revelation of John, Yeshua sends a message to the church. People who only have a little bit of strength are receiving the overwhelmingly gracious gifts of the Lord. If you don't feel very strong right now, consider what the Lord is saying to you in Joel 3:10b, *"Let the weak say, 'I am strong."*

With the authority given to you by Yeshua, you can speak strength into existence for yourself right now. Think about this as you read the letter Yeshua wrote for us in the passage below. Also, consider the added condition of standing with Him and not denying His name.

> *I know your works. See, I have set before you an open door, and no one can shut it; for you have a little strength, have kept My word, and have not denied My name.* (Revelation 3:8)

The Lord knows that we are living in perilous times (For more on this idea see my book: Alert! Perilous Times). Even if you live in the place where Satan has an established throne, you can receive all His precious promises. Even if you are barely holding it together and if you are standing on a shaky faith, He can do His mighty works for you. The key to understanding this principle is to realize that He will do what He has promised because it is for you, but He will also do it for His name's sake. The key here is to hold fast to His name and avoid denying your faith in Him. Hold on to what He promised the church in the passage below:

> *I know where you dwell, where Satan's throne is. Yet you hold fast my name, and you did not deny my faith even in the days of Antipas my faithful witness, who was killed among you, where Satan dwells.* (Revelation 2:13, ESV)

Through the prophet Isaiah, the Lord revealed all He had done and will do for His people even if they have transgressed and are guilty of sin. He blots all of it out. The imagery here is from a past era when writers would use a blotter to wipe away the mistakes they made. The Lord has the big blotter and for His name's sake, He is willing to blot from the record all your past failures. Then the Lord promises what is logically impossible. God the Father chooses to forget our sins and failures. He knows everything but has the power to forget what He does not want to remember about your past. Consider all the Lord has done for you as you study the passage below. Then think about how little He is asking of you. I don't know about you, but I am filled right now with gratitude as I overflow in thankfulness, praise, and glory to Him and for Him.

> *I, even I, am He who blots out your transgressions* **for My own sake***; and I will not remember your sins. Put Me in remembrance; let us contend together; state your case, that you may be acquitted. Your first father sinned, and your mediators have transgressed against Me. Therefore I will profane the princes of the sanctuary; I will give Jacob to the curse, and Israel to reproaches.* (Isaiah 43:25-28)

IMPORTANCE OF GUARDING HIS NAME

What is so important about guarding the Lord's name? Think about it. All these glorious promises are based on this powerful name. The key to receiving, activating, and living under the glorious promises of the Lord is to let them bring glory to Him and His name. It isn't all that complicated. He didn't offer something and then cloak it in mystery. He didn't make it nearly impossible for us to discover what He can and will do for us. He boldly stated the promises and clearly explained what we need to do to receive these gifts, blessings, and grace which He has promised. To make it as clear as possible, I have listed some of the reasons why guarding and protecting His name is so important for you and me.

1. HIS NAME IS HOLY

> *So I will make My holy name known in the midst of My people Israel, and I will not let them profane My holy name anymore. Then the nations shall know that I am the Lord, the Holy One in Israel.* (Ezekiel 39:7)

The fact that His name is holy is a sufficient reason to jealously guard and protect it, but there is so much more. If you belong to Him, He will work to help prevent you from profaning His name. Some people choose to look at this promise from a negative perspective. They see this and think that the Lord is preventing them from doing something they want to be free to act on in their own lives. On the other hand, I look at this from a positive perspective. The Lord is providing safeguards so that we will not accidentally do the wrong thing. This is a gift from the Lord to help us stay close to Him and live in a way that brings honor and glory to Him.

Jesus answered and said, "This voice came not because of me, but for your sakes. Now is the judgment of this world: now shall the prince of this world be cast out. And I, if I be lifted up from the earth, will draw all men unto me." (John 12:30-32, KJV)

Think about it this way: One of the reasons He is enabling us to be faithful is so that we can safeguard His precious name. He is doing this because He has a great plan which is already in motion. He is allowing us to participate in a great move of God for the nations. He is planning to act through us in a way that will draw all people to Him. He is paying the majority of the cost and is only asking a little from us. Remember what Yeshua said in the passage above, *"This voice came not because of me, but for your sakes."* He is doing all this for you, and through you for others.

2. HIS NAME IS POWERFUL

And His name, through faith in His name, has made this man strong, whom you see and know. Yes, the faith which comes through Him has given him this perfect soundness in the presence of you all. (Acts 3:16)

The Lord's name has the power to overcome sickness, infirmity, and weakness in our spirits, souls, and bodies. How would you like to experience *"perfect soundness"* in your entire body? Think about it. There is power in the name and all you have to do is trust Him. All that is required is for you to have "*faith in His name.*" Remember that this faith is also a gift from the Lord. He gives us faith and then gives us more faith. We may only have faith the size of a mustard seed, but the Lord can magnify and multiply it so that mountains will be moved and bodies will be healed. Don't look at the size of your faith. Look at the size of His love, grace, and power.

He releases power when we reverently use His name. He gives the power to release the remission of sin and to restore the spirits and souls of His suffering children. Think about the spiritual power which he releases to us through that name: "*But as many as received him, to them gave he power to become the sons of God, even to them that believe on his name:*" (John 1:12, KJV). There are things in the spiritual realm that require great power to be activated. We often miss this, because we are more clearly focused on the natural realm. Consider this as you study the passage below. Have you received this power? Receive it. Activate it. Let it manifest in your life and ministry. Amen?

> *And He commanded us to preach to the people, and to testify that it is He who was ordained by God to be Judge of the living and the dead. To Him all the prophets witness that, <u>through His name,</u> whoever believes in Him will receive remission of sins.*" (Acts 10:42-43)

3. HIS REPUTATION IS ESSENTIAL

Let this mind be in you which was also in Christ Jesus, who, being in the form of God, did not consider it robbery to be equal with God, but made Himself of no reputation, taking the form of a bondservant, and coming in the likeness of men. And being found in appearance as a man, He humbled Himself and became obedient to the point of death, even the death of the cross. Therefore God also has highly exalted Him and given Him the name which is above every name, that at the name of Jesus every knee should bow, of those in heaven, and of those on earth, and of those under the earth, and that every tongue should confess that Jesus Christ is Lord, to the glory of God the Father. (Philippians 2:5-11)

The passage above is a little long, but I couldn't find a good place to stop because it is all so critical to what we are considering here. He gave up His amazing and awesome reputation to come into unity with us. This is truly amazing when we take time to consider the impact of this gift from the Lord. He came down so far and humbled Himself in obedience even to death on the cross to bring us back up to the place Father God has for us. I am so thankful for what He did and for what He still does for us.

When we come to Him in faith, another great spiritual miracle happens. He receives back the glory and honor He so richly deserves. Because of His work in us, He gets His reputation back. He receives such an amazing elevation that at His name every knee will bow and every tongue will confess that Yeshua ha Messiach is Adonai. When this happens for Him, it releases something else in the spiritual realm. It brings glory to the name of God the Father. All is restored in this amazing move of God. We see the results of this powerful transformation when the Lord speaks: "*Then He who sat on the throne said, 'Behold, I make all things new.'*" (Revelation 21:5) You are invited to be a part of this amazing move of the Lord. Are you ready for it?

4. OUR PROTECTOR RESPECTED

When I shut up heaven and there is no rain, or command the locusts to devour the land, or send pestilence among My people, if My people who are called by My name will humble themselves, and pray and seek My face, and turn from their wicked ways, then I will hear from heaven, and will forgive their sin and heal their land. (2 Chronicals7:13-14)

Our reputations are tied together. The Lord's people are called by His name. If His reputation is tarnished, ours will also be profaned. We need to be in unity with Him to receive all He has promised. We need to be the guardians of His name and the defenders of His reputation. This unity is the key to moving with the Lord in His next great awakening. It is the key to releasing His promises in our lives. It is the key to making our prayers effective. When we humble ourselves in obedience as Yeshua did, the way is opened for the release of His power to forgive and heal our people and our land. Amen?

BENEFITS OF HIS NAME

Below I have gathered some of the passages of scripture which demonstrate the benefits we receive through His name. This list is not exhaustive. It is a beginning. As you continue in your Bible study, begin to notice the benefits you receive from knowing, respecting, and honoring His glorious name. As you study these passages reflect on what the Lord is doing in your life and work. The Lord doesn't sugarcoat these things. He lets us know that there is a price that must be paid.

1. YOU ARE A CHOSEN VESSEL

(Ask the Holy Spirit to reveal it to you.)

But the Lord said to him, "Go, for he is a chosen vessel of Mine to bear My name before Gentiles, kings, and the children of Israel. For I will show him how many things he must suffer for My name's sake." (Acts 9:15-16)

2. HEALING AND PROVISON

But to you who fear My name the Sun of Righteousness shall arise with healing in His wings; and you shall go out and grow fat like stall-fed calves. (Malachi 4:2)

3. YOU HAVE A PURPOSE IN THE KINGDOM

For the Scripture says to the Pharaoh, "For this very purpose I have raised you up, that I may show My power in you, and that My name may be declared in all the earth." Therefore He has mercy on whom He wills, and whom He wills He hardens. (Romans 9:17-18)

4. THE LORD ANSWERS HIS PEOPLE

I will bring the one-third through the fire, will refine them as silver is refined, and test them as gold is tested. They will call on My name, and I will answer them. I will say, 'This is My people'; and each one will say, 'The Lord is my God. (Zechariah 13:9)

DANGER IN PROFANING THE NAME

I will send out the curse," says the Lord of hosts; "It shall enter the house of the thief and the house of the one who swears falsely by My name. It shall remain in the midst of his house and consume it, with its timber and stones." (Zechariah 5:4)

I would be remiss if I didn't share what the Lord says about those who choose to profane His name. There are two very powerful truths being released through the Word of the Lord in this generation. Great blessing and favor are being released to those who are faithful and obedient in this season. For those willing to be led by the Lord, a great season of restoration has been decreed. Those who are willing can receive it, activate it, and receive all that the Lord has promised. But for those who will not believe and receive His gifts; for those who choose to profane His name, a great season of judgment is being released. It is the Lord's desire for you to choose life, restoration, blessing, and favor, but He leaves that decision up to you and me. What will you choose?

> *Then you turned around and profaned My name, and every one of you brought back his male and female slaves, whom he had set at liberty, at their pleasure, and brought them back into subjection, to be your male and female slaves.* (Jeremiah 34:16)

At this point, I began to reflect on a question that was recurring in my mind: What will be released on those who profane His name. These things are revealed in the scriptures, but many people have chosen to ignore them. A manmade doctrine holds that a loving God will not punish his wayward children. This is the opposite of the teaching in the Word of God. It is not the time to sugarcoat it or try to bring in people who do not accept their responsibility to honor and obey the Lord. I found several clear statements about these things and share them with you below.

1. SHAME SHALL BE UPON THEM

Hear the word of the Lord, you who tremble at His word: "Your brethren who hated you, who cast you out for My name's sake, said, 'Let the Lord be glorified, that we may see your joy.' But they shall be ashamed." (Isaiah 66:5)

2. DISHONORING GOD RESULTS IN DISHONOR FOR US

But I acted for My name's sake, that it should not be profaned before the Gentiles among whom they were, in whose sight I had made Myself known to them, to bring them out of the land of Egypt. (Ezekiel 20:9)

3. EXCLUDED FROM THE PROMISED LAND AND HIS REST

But I acted for My name's sake, that it should not be profaned before the Gentiles, in whose sight I had brought them out. So I also raised My hand in an oath to them in the wilderness, that I would not bring them into the land which I had given them, 'flowing with milk and honey,' the glory of all lands, because they despised My judgments and did not walk in My statutes, but profaned My Sabbaths; for their heart went after their idols. (Ezekiel 20:14-16)

4. THE LORD WITHDRAWS HIS HAND

Nevertheless I withdrew My hand and acted for My name's sake, that it should not be profaned in the sight of the Gentiles, in whose sight I had brought them out. (Ezekiel 20:22)

5. HE CHANGES HOW HE DEALS WITH YOU

Then you shall know that I am the Lord, when I have dealt with you for My name's sake, not according to your wicked ways nor according to your corrupt doings, O house of Israel, says the Lord God. (Ezekiel 20:44)

BLESSINGS FOR HONORING HIS NAME

But before all these things, they will lay their hands on you and persecute you, delivering you up to the synagogues and prisons. You will be brought before kings and rulers for My name's sake. (Luke 21:12)

The passage above is not the end of the story. What you have received from the Lord cannot be taken away by the world. Regardless of how dire the circumstances may look, all that the Lord has given you is protected in eternity. In the passages below, I share some of the great promises of the Lord for those who remain faithful and honor His name through their witness, service, and example. The outcome in the present may not seem very attractive, but the promises in the spiritual realm are eternal and awesome. The Lord wants to bless you and give you all the promised blessings of eternal life. We may have to endure for a season, but the blessings are forever. Amen?

1. BECOMING HIS CHOSEN VESSEL

But the Lord said to him, "Go, for he is a chosen vessel of Mine to bear My name before Gentiles, kings, and the children of Israel. For I will show him how many things he must suffer for My name's sake." (Acts 9:15-16)

2. ENDURING RESULTS IN SALVATION (triple witness)

And you will be hated by all for My name's sake. But he who endures to the end will be saved. (Matthew 10:22)

Then they will deliver you up to tribulation and kill you, and you will be hated by all nations for My name's sake. (Matthew 24:9)

And you will be hated by all for My name's sake. But he who endures to the end shall be saved. (Mark 13:13)

3. PROVISION FOR NOW AND ETERNITY

And everyone who has left houses or brothers or sisters or father or mother or wife or children or lands, for My name's sake, shall receive a hundredfold, and inherit eternal life. But many who are first will be last, and the last first. (Matthew 19:29-30)

4. PATIENCE RELEASES POWER OF PROTECTION

You will be betrayed even by parents and brothers, relatives and friends; and they will put some of you to death. And you will be hated by all for My name's sake. But not a hair of your head shall be lost. By your patience possess your souls. (Luke 21:16-19)

AVOID FALSE TEACHING

I remember a form of evangelism being taught when I was a youth which was based on manmade doctrine rather than the Word of the Lord. According to this false teaching, those who accepted Yeshua would suddenly have all their problems taken away and they would live free from hardship, lack, criticism, and hard times of service. It was a kind of "pie in the sky" approach to persuading people to accept Yeshua. The problem with maintaining this idea was that people almost immediately experienced trouble, sorrow, loss, and painful attacks.

This was like the seed planted on the path or the seed which fell on the rock. These evangelistic seeds didn't have time to take root before they were taken away. The loss to the kingdom was great because it was almost impossible to get these people to turn to the Lord again. Yeshua didn't call people this way. He made it clear that they would be challenged. The passage below from John is very clear about this. Yeshua suffered and He proved Himself by being faithful through it. If He suffered, how can we expect to be treated well if we are doing the things He did and saying the things He said? Think about it and pray for wisdom and understanding as you process this teaching.

> *Remember the word that I said to you, 'A servant is not greater than his master.' If they persecuted Me, they will also persecute you. If they kept My word, they will keep yours also. But all these things they will do to you for My name's sake, because they do not know Him who sent Me.* (John 15:20-21)

Don't be misled. The Lord knows our works and He understands fully how firmly we are committed to Him. It is not enough to merely do some good works. If you lose your first love, none of your good works will matter. We understand that Yeshua is calling our love and commitment to Him our "first love." Don't give up! Don't even think about quitting. Be fully committed to Him and never let go.

> *I know your works, your labor, your patience, and that you cannot bear those who are evil. And you have tested those who say they are apostles and*

are not, and have found them liars; and you have persevered and have patience, and have labored for My name's sake and have not become weary. Nevertheless I have this against you, that you have left your first love. (Revelation 2:2-4)

ACTIVATION

The Lord does not always act simply because we want Him to do something for us. At times He acts to protect His name and reputation. This is what He did when Hezekiah prayed an activation prayer as recorded in Second Kings. Hezekiah was praying for his own sake and the sake of his people, but the Lord said He activated the promise to avoid profaning His name. He did it to continue to fulfill His previous promises to David and those who lived in later generations.

As we activate His promises, we need to put aside our self-seeking and egocentric ways of thinking and praying. Consider this as you study the passage below from one of Israel's great kings. On the surface, it seems that Hezekiah is acting appropriately to the Lord, but soon afterward He became ill. The Lord sent Isaiah to him once more to let him know that he was going to die from this illness. He wept and cried out to the Lord and Isaiah was sent back to him with news that the Lord would heal him and these perilous times would happen after his lifetime. This is where his self-centeredness is revealed. You can find this in 2 Kings 20:19, *"So Hezekiah said to Isaiah,*

'The word of the Lord which you have spoken is good!'" For he said, "Will there not be peace and truth at least in my days?"

> And Hezekiah received the letter from the hand of the messengers, and read it; and Hezekiah went up to the house of the Lord, and spread it before the Lord. Then Hezekiah prayed before the Lord, and said: "O Lord God of Israel, the One who dwells between the cherubim, You are God, You alone, of all the kingdoms of the earth. You have made heaven and earth. Incline Your ear, O Lord, and hear; open Your eyes, O Lord, and see; and hear the words of Sennacherib, which he has sent to reproach the living God. Truly, Lord, the kings of Assyria have laid waste the nations and their lands, and have cast their gods into the fire; for they were not gods, but the work of men's hands—wood and stone. Therefore they destroyed them. Now therefore, O Lord our God, I pray, save us from his hand, that all the kingdoms of the earth may know that You are the Lord God, You alone." (2 Kings 19:14-19)

> Then Isaiah the son of Amoz sent to Hezekiah, saying, "Thus says the Lord God of Israel: 'Because you have prayed to Me against Sennacherib king of Assyria, I have heard.' This is the word which the Lord has spoken concerning him: (2 Kings 19:20-21a)

The Lord had some "I will" statements of judgment for the Babylonian king, Sennacherib. He had profaned the name of the Lord over and over. He had boasted of his power to do as he pleased with the Lord's people. He believed and stated that the Lord had no power over him. He brutally oppressed and savagely murdered many people in his quest for power. This was the time for the Lord to demonstrate His power and control over this and every other situation. The tables were being turned and Sennacherib was getting back what he had done against so many others. Who can save from the hand of the Lord?

> *But I know your dwelling place, your going out and your coming in, and your rage against Me. Because your rage against Me and your tumult have come up to My ears, therefore **I will** put My hook in your nose and My bridle in your lips, and **I will** turn you back by the way which you came.* (2 Kings 19:27-28)

> *Therefore thus says the Lord concerning the king of Assyria: "He shall not come into this city, nor shoot an arrow there, nor come before it with shield, nor build a siege mound against it. By the way that he came, by the same shall he return; and he shall not come into this city," says the Lord. "For **I will** defend this city, to save it for My own sake and for My servant David's sake."* (2 Kings 19:32-34)

Hezekiah activated the Lord's promises by humbling himself and praying for the help of the Lord. This is similar to the way David activated the Lord's promises in the past. This was not the only way of reaching out to receive what the Lord had promised. David constantly sought the presence of the Lord and appealed to Him on many different levels and in many varied ways. Below you can see another way David Activated the Lord's promises.

But You, O God the Lord, deal with me for Your name's sake; because Your mercy is good, deliver me. (Psalm 109:21)

In this case, David did not appeal based on His merit. His request was based on an appeal for the Lord to do what would uphold His *"name's sake"*. What does this mean for you and me? Those who stand with the Lord also stand under His protective covering. When the Father moves to uphold His name, all those who call upon that name reap the benefits of His work. Lining up with the Lord lines you up under His blessing and favor and opens up all His promises of redemption, restoration, and protection for you. Consider how this works in the passage below.

Help me, O Lord my God! Oh, save me according to Your mercy, that they may know that this is Your hand—that You, Lord, have done it! Let them curse, but You bless; when they arise, let them be ashamed, but let Your servant rejoice. Let my accusers be clothed with shame, and let them cover themselves with their own disgrace as with a mantle. I will greatly praise the Lord with my mouth; Yes, I will praise Him among the multitude. For He shall stand at the right hand of the poor, to save him from those who condemn him. (Psalm 109:26-31)

NAME'S SAKE SCRIPTURES

I encourage you to study the Word of God and discover for yourself more of His work which was and is being done for His name's sake. To help you begin, I am providing several of the powerful teachings in the Word. Each one carries unique and powerful ways in which this work of the Lord can benefit you. You probably know many more and can add to this list now. You can also benefit from studying the Word of God to receive and activate these promises and blessings in your own life and ministry.

1. A POWERFUL MOVE OF REDEMPTION

But I acted for My name's sake, that it should not be profaned before the Gentiles among whom they were, in whose sight I had made Myself known to them, to bring them out of the land of Egypt. (Ezekiel 20:9)

2. AVOID BEING LEFT OUT

But I acted for My name's sake, that it should not be profaned before the Gentiles, in whose sight I had brought them out. So I also raised My hand in an oath to them in the wilderness, that I would not bring them into the land which I had given them, 'flowing with milk and honey,' the glory of all lands, because they despised My judgments and did not walk in My statutes, but profaned My Sabbaths; for their heart went after their idols. (Ezekiel 20:14-16)

3. RELEASES UNMERITED GRACE

Notwithstanding, the children rebelled against Me; they did not walk in My statutes, and were not careful to observe My judgments, 'which, if a man does, he shall live by them'; but they profaned My Sabbaths. Then I said I would pour out My fury on them and fulfill My anger against them in the wilderness. Nevertheless I withdrew My hand and acted for My name's sake, that it should not be profaned in the sight of the Gentiles, in whose sight I had brought them out. (Ezekiel 20:21-22)

4. GET TO KNOW THE LORD

Then you shall know that I am the Lord, when I have dealt with you for My name's sake, not according to your wicked ways nor according to your corrupt doings, O house of Israel," says the Lord God. (Ezekiel 20:44)

5. HALLOWED FOR HIS NAME'S SAKE

Therefore say to the house of Israel, "Thus says the Lord God: 'I do not do this for your sake, O house of

Israel, but for My holy name's sake, which you have profaned among the nations wherever you went. And I will sanctify My great name, which has been profaned among the nations, which you have profaned in their midst; and the nations shall know that I am the Lord," says the Lord God, *"when I am hallowed in you before their eyes."* (Ezekiel 36:22-23)

6. REVELATION INCREASES AS HIS NAME IS HONORED

Therefore thus says the Lord God: 'Now I will bring back the captives of Jacob, and have mercy on the whole house of Israel; and I will be jealous for My holy name—after they have borne their shame, and all their unfaithfulness in which they were unfaithful to Me, when they dwelt safely in their own land and no one made them afraid. When I have brought them back from the peoples and gathered them out of their enemies' lands, and I am hallowed in them in the sight of many nations, then they shall know that I am the Lord their God, who sent them into captivity among the nations, but also brought them back to their land, and left none of them captive any longer. And I will not hide My face from them anymore; for I shall have poured out My Spirit on the house of Israel,' says the Lord God." (Ezekiel 39:25-29)

SELAH QUESTIONS

(Selah means to pause and meditate on these things.)

1. Whose responsibility is it to protect the name of the Lord?

_____

_____

_____

2. What is so important about guarding the Lord's name?

_____

_____

_____

3. Name two benefits of upholding the name of the Lord.

_____

_____

_____

4. What are the potential costs of profaning the name of the Lord?

_____

_____

_____

5. What are some of the ways the Lord blesses those who honor His name?

_____

_____

_____

6. How did Hezekiah limit his blessing from the Lord?

_____

_____

_____

CHAPTER TWELVE

Double Portion Restoration

At that time I will gather you; at that time I will bring you home. I will give you honor and praise among all the peoples of the earth when I restore your fortunes before your very eyes, (Zephaniah 3:20, NIV)

Good news! A grand time of restoration is coming and it has already started to manifest. The really good news is that the promises were not just for the people living in the time in which it was given. It is also for you and me. We are receiving the Lord's promised restoration now and more is to come in the future. It was through the prophet, Zephaniah, that we received these amazing and comforting promises from the Lord. Once the Word of God is released, it does not just go away. We can take comfort in the permanence of the Lord's promises. But even all these wonderful and powerful benefits are not the end of the message. Remember that the Lord always gives more and more.

In addition to its release in previous generations, it is still available to be released again in another generation. I want to release it in this generation. How about you? Think about it. Here are three more "I will" promises of restoration for us to receive and activate. Do you long for the Lord to gather His people, bring them home, and give them honor and praise in front of all people? Do you long to have the Lord restore everything to you right in front of your own eyes? If you answered yes to one or more of these questions, then these promises of restoration are for you.

Most people like the idea of restoration. What do you think of when you hear the word restoration? Most, if not all of us, have lost something in the past which we would like to have back. As you consider what you have lost and want to have restored, be aware that these promises include the restoration of things lost in the spiritual realm as well as things lost in the natural realm. Last year I received a word from the Lord that many people would receive their God-given inheritance back even long after the Yovel (Year of Jubilee). These things included but were not limited to things that had been lost or stolen in a previous generation of their families. I believe that word is still valid today. Have you lost part or all of your inheritance? Now is the time to ask the Lord to restore it for you as you prepare yourself to receive all He has promised to you. Now is the time to activate all these powerful promises in your own life and ministry.

Are you ready to step forward and receive the valuable things you have lost in the past? Take a moment and think about something you have lost which you sincerely desire to have once again. When the Lord decrees restoration are you among those who quickly get in line to receive it back? I am always ready for a time (or better yet a season) of restoration. How about you? As you reflect on the Lord's plan for restoration, it becomes clear that His promises are more oriented toward releasing a season rather than just one item. The Lord doesn't do small thinking. He thinks big and He acts in an even bigger way. Trust Him to release powerful and plentiful restoration in your life, in your family, and your ministry.

As I mentioned earlier, I have noticed that in conferences and spiritual meetings, people tend to get excited about the idea of restoration. If an impartation of restoration is offered, most people in the meetings rush forward to get in line. The reality is that most, if not all of us have experienced some painful losses in the past. If you are fully aware of what you desire to have restored, you are more likely to receive it. As you think about it, remember that the Lord has a larger plan in mind than what you are considering.

Remember how Paul described this aspect of the Lord's character in Ephesians 3:20-21, "*Now to Him who is able to do exceedingly abundantly above all that we ask or think, according to the power that works in us, to Him be glory in the church by Christ Jesus to all generations, forever and ever. Amen.*" The Lord is not only able but willing to give so generously to you. You are His child. He created you for a purpose and He wants you to have all you need to succeed in and for His Kingdom. This is your destiny. Embrace it now and ask to receive everything you need to accomplish all He has planned for you. Amen? As you can see, the main question is: are you ready and willing to receive it?

As I mentioned above, I often teach these things in meetings. Then I begin to refer to the double portion promises, blessings, and gifts of the Lord. When I do this many people get even more excited to receive what the Lord has for them. Most people in spiritual meetings get excited when reference is made to receiving any kind of "double portion" blessing. To fully appreciate this I wanted to dig deeper to get at all it means for you and me. I invite you now to consider with me some things which go beyond the surface. First think about what it means in the context of Bible times. In other words, what does a double portion mean from a Biblical point of view? I began to research this idea and found that it can mean a variety of different things depending on the circumstances of His people when the Lord gives the release.

RESTORATION IN THE NATURAL

And the Lord restored Job's losses when he prayed for his friends. Indeed the Lord gave Job twice as much as he had before. (Job 42:10)

In the natural realm, what do you need from the Lord? What would you like to ask Him to restore in your life and/or ministry? Think about this: is it appropriate to ask the Lord to restore these natural things? The quick answer is "Yes!" The

Lord makes this kind of double portion blessing clear for us in the book of Job. Job lost everything except his complaining wife. *"Then his wife said to him, 'Do you still hold fast to your integrity? Curse God and die!'"* (Job 2:9) But who among us can blame her, she lost everything in the same way Job did. Her children were gone. Her prosperity and provision had been lost. Can you imagine the anger and resentment building in her spirit and soul? Any mother who has lost a child knows all too well how that pain feels and how deeply it penetrates your heart; even to the deepest parts of your soul.

Perhaps you have lost something so valuable that you have difficulty moving on as you continue to feel the intense pain of loss. You may be very personally and intimately aware of the depth of pain felt by Job's wife. In times like this, it is hard to believe that there is any hope left. It may seem that all is lost. But with the Lord, there is always hope. Remember the words of the angel to Elizabeth in Luke 1:37 (NIV), *"For nothing is impossible with God."* Do you believe this? Then also consider what Yeshua said to a father asking for his son's healing. *"Jesus said to him, "If you can believe, all things are possible to him who believes."* (Mark 9:23) Let this be a prophetic word for you. Trust the Lord not only for restoration but for a double portion restoration in your life. In the passage below we look back once again to the story of Job and the restoration of a double portion in his life.

> *And his sons would go and feast in their houses, each on his appointed day, and would send and invite their three sisters to eat and drink with them.*

So it was, when the days of feasting had run their course, that Job would send and sanctify them, and he would rise early in the morning and offer burnt offerings according to the number of them all. For Job said, "It may be that my sons have sinned and cursed God in their hearts." Thus Job did regularly. (Job 1:4-5)

For Job, the experience of pain, loss, and fear were even more intense because his loss was something he had feared for a long time. Remember what he said in Job 3:25, *"For the thing I greatly feared has come upon me, and what I dreaded has happened to me."* What was his fear? He didn't have the assurance of the salvation of his children. Many people can identify with this fear. Job had no confidence that his children were right in their relationship with the Lord. It was his greatest fear that they would die and be lost. He had this intense fear when they were alive and now he carried this terrible burden after their deaths. Job didn't need a double portion of that pain and fear. He didn't need more of the abuse He had taken from his wife in her pain. Therefore, the Lord didn't give Job a double portion of wives or children.

What we learn from this is that when the Lord doubles our portion in His restoration it is only for the things which will bless us and give us a positive increase. Think about what the Lord is saying to you in Psalm 115:13, *"He will bless those who fear the Lord, both small and great."* Think about it. When you are right with God, He blesses you with increase more and more. Consider Psalm 115:14-15, *"May the Lord give you increase more and more, you and your children. May you be blessed by the Lord, Who made heaven and earth."* Receive it right now and activate it in your life. Be very encouraged that it is also released for your family and your ministry right now. Amen? Always be careful to give the Lord the praise and glory He is due for being so good to us.

THE POWER OF HOPE

*Return to the stronghold, you prisoners of hope. Even today I declare that **I will restore double** to you. For I have bent Judah, My bow, fitted the bow with Ephraim, and raised up your sons, O Zion, against your sons, O Greece, and made you like the sword of a mighty man." Then the Lord will be seen over them, and His arrow will go forth like lightning. The Lord God will blow the trumpet, and go with whirlwinds from the south. The Lord of hosts will defend them; They shall devour and subdue with slingstones. They shall drink and roar as if with wine; they shall be filled with blood like basins, like the corners of the altar. The Lord their God will save them in that day, as the flock of His people. For they shall be like the jewels of a crown, lifted like a banner over His land*—(Zechariah 9:12-16)

When things and people who are close to you are lost or stolen, don't give up hope. The Lord is the source of your restoration and the source of your hope. Trust Him and believe for all the valuable things you have lost to come back to you as an awesome gift from the Lord. I once had a very powerful spiritual experience related to things that have been lost. In a vision, I was carried by the Spirit to a very unusual room in Heaven. The place was lined with small boxes and drawers. Even the pillars in the room had small drawers attached to them. There was a man in the room (perhaps an angel). He asked me if I wanted something back. It was then that I was told by the Spirit that this heavenly being was the keeper of lost things.

The keeper then opened a small drawer near the wall. I looked in and saw my childhood treasures which I thought had been long lost. I was very glad to see them, but I didn't have a use for them at that time. So I left them in the drawer. I knew there was something about this experience which was much greater than having those old lost treasures returned. I understood that this little object lesson was given to assure me and you that nothing small or great is ever lost in the spiritual realm. Everything is protected and waiting for the right moment to be restored. Be expectant in this season of restoration. Be ready to see valuable things and old treasures returned to you. Be ready for a double portion restoration in your life. Amen?

FIRST SON'S PORTION

Now I want to take you a step deeper into the understanding of the truth about biblical double portion restoration. You also need to be aware that there is a spiritual meaning attached to the idea of a "double portion" restoration by the Lord. A double portion can symbolize love and affection as it did in the life of a woman named Hannah. *"But to Hannah he would give a double portion, for he loved Hannah, although the Lord had closed her womb."* (1 Samuel 1:5) The spiritual truth is that the Lord often gives a double portion of His grace to reassure us of His love, appreciation, and provision. Hannah's husband, Elkanah, demonstrated the depth of his love for Hannah by always giving her a double portion. From this biblical story, we learn of the deep love and grace the Lord also pours out for us in a double portion blessing. Why does He do it? For the same reason that Elkanah did it. It is because of His love for us. Amen?

The promises of the Lord were also given to the children of some of the characters in the Bible. Notice the "something else" which is established in Deuteronomy 21:17, *"But he shall acknowledge the son of the unloved wife as the firstborn by giving him a double portion of all that he has, for he is the beginning of his strength; the right of the firstborn is his."* This is a powerful affirmation and promise for people who have not been blessed with the right kind of love and affection from their natural parents or other people who had authority over them. The Lord wants you to know something very special. No matter what people have done to you or withheld from you, the Lord will give you the double portion blessing of a firstborn child. Don't let your circumstances or doubts determine what you can receive from the Lord. Believe for more. Expect more. This prepares your heart and soul to receive more of what the Lord wants to restore to you. Amen?

And so it was, when they had crossed over, that Elijah said to Elisha, "Ask! What may I do for you, before I am taken away from you?" Elisha said, "Please let a double portion of your spirit be upon me." (2 Kings 2:9)

I think there has been some confusion about the passage above. Some people have told me this has to do with the number of miracles performed by each of these two prophets. I don't look at it this way. Those who say this have to count one thing which happened after Elisha had died and after he had been buried for many years. There is a deeper meaning to the fulfillment of this request. Consider this, both prophets (Elijah and Elisha) did many things that were not recorded in scripture. Who knows how many miracles each of them released by the power of God? There is no way to mathematically figure out what Elisha was asking in the passage above.

Now consider this, Elisha was asking to receive a powerful spiritual blessing and a unique anointing. He was asking to be like the firstborn son of Elijah. This status would provide many things for him when he received his inheritance. He would be the leader of the companies of the prophets. He would not only be recognized as their official leader but would also be established as their teacher, mentor, and guide. A double portion from Elijah would have been understood this way in the culture of their times.

Elisha also needed an extra portion of power and authority to complete a mission that the Lord had given to Elijah. In his lifetime, Elijah was never able to complete all of the tasks which the Lord had assigned to him. Elisha had to have the spiritual strength to take on Jezebel and to anoint kings for both Israel and Judah. We are told that this request was honored by the Lord. Spiritual authority came from the Lord to Elisha as it would have been given to the firstborn son of Elijah. With this double portion blessing, Elisha completed those tasks given to Elijah and went on to accomplish so much more for the Kingdom of God.

The Lord's double portion also affirms your position and importance in the Kingdom. We are taught in scripture that when we accept Yeshua as our Lord and Savior, we are accepted and loved as He is loved by Father God. Through Yeshua, we are given a relationship with Father God as it is with His firstborn, Yeshua ha Messiach. This is such an awesome thought. How can it be? It is true because the Lord has promised the double portion (firstborn portion) to all of us, and He always keeps His promises. Don't let doubts or unresolved guilt keep you from receiving what the Lord wants to release to you right now. Amen?

The double portion is also given for another reason. In the past, it was given to break off the shame and disgrace of the Lord's people. It can also be given for the same reason in this present time. The same amazing gifts of the Lord are for the generation of those who have been redeemed of the Lord. When people are restored with a double portion, their status with the Lord becomes clear. They are loved and blessed with His favor. After all, who can argue with the double portion blessing or against those who receive it? It is an obvious sign of the Lord's grace, favor, and blessing. It does even more than the release of grace in the present. It also produces an everlasting joy for those who receive it. Could you use a little "everlasting joy" in your life right now? Read the passage below aloud and receive it for yourself. Then activate it according to the Word of God.

> *Instead of their shame my people will receive a double portion, and instead of disgrace they will rejoice in their inheritance; and so they will inherit a double portion in their land, and everlasting joy will be theirs.* (Isaiah 61:7)

DOUBLE PORTION JUDGMENT

There is another type of double portion which most of us don't want to consider, but it is one of the truths released in God's Word. The Lord occasionally gives a double portion of the judgment. If you wonder if that is something you are experiencing, let me assure you that it isn't. If you are seeking to make things right with the Lord, you are not in line for this kind of judgment. People who receive this double portion have been given over to a debased and fleshly mind which no longer considers accountability or repentance. The Lord has shown them over and over, but they will not see. He has sent prophetic messages many times, but they will not listen. He put it in His Word and they will not read it or believe it.

Then I heard another voice from heaven say: "Come out of her, my people, so that you will not share in her sins, so that you will not receive any of her plagues; for her sins are piled up to heaven, and God has remembered her crimes. Give back to her as she has given; pay her back double for what she has done. Mix her a double portion from her own cup. (Revelation 18:4-6, NIV)

In the last days, when final judgment is rendered, this kind of double portion will be given to people, groups, and nations because of their apostasy from Father God. I call this "final jeopardy." This kind of judgment is for people who have brought great pain and unjustified persecution on the Lord's anointed people. At the end of the age, all things will be made right with those who have come to the Lord through a saving faith in Yeshua ha Messiach. In the meantime, we continue to pray in intercession for others who are in danger. We do this without judging them. Judging is not our job. The Lord will be the judge then as He is now.

Judge not, that you be not judged. For with what judgment you judge, you will be judged; and with the measure you use, it will be measured back to you. And why do you look at the speck in your brother's eye, but do not consider the plank in your own eye? Or how can you say to your brother, 'Let me remove the speck from your eye'; and look, a plank is in your own eye? Hypocrite! First remove the plank from your own eye, and then you will see clearly to remove the speck from your brother's eye. (Matthew 7:1-5)

RESTORATION PRAYERS

We often see the release of great gifts of the Lord for the restoration of His people during His true revival movements. Psalm 85 has often been used as the foundational prayer of the people during a revival. They often cry out: "*Will You not revive us again, that Your people may rejoice in You?*" (Psalm 85:6) Perhaps you have prayed these same words during a time of revival in your life. I pray to the Lord now "*Restore us, O God of our salvation, and cause Your anger toward us to cease.*" (Psalm 85:4) Are you praying yet? Now is the time to release our appeals to Him once again. Now is the time to cry out for a double portion of His love, grace, forgiveness, and mercy. Think about it as you pray the whole Psalm 85 prayer below. Remember that reading things aloud releases the Word of God in your life and ministry.

> *Lord, You have been favorable to Your land; You have brought back the captivity of Jacob. You have forgiven the iniquity of Your people; You have covered all their sin. Selah You have taken away all Your wrath; You have turned from the fierceness of Your anger. Will You be angry with us forever? Will You prolong Your anger to all generations? Will You not revive us again, that Your people may rejoice in You? Show us Your mercy, Lord, and grant us*

Your salvation. I will hear what God the Lord will speak, for He will speak peace to His people and to His saints; but let them not turn back to folly. Surely His salvation is near to those who fear Him, that glory may dwell in our land. Mercy and truth have met together; righteousness and peace have kissed. Truth shall spring out of the earth, and righteousness shall look down from heaven. Yes, the Lord will give what is good; and our land will yield its increase. Righteousness will go before Him, and shall make His footsteps our pathway. (Psalm 85)

INTERCESSION FOR RESTORATION

Another great source of prayer for restoration is Psalm 74. In the first two verses, the psalmist cries out: "*O God, why have You cast us off forever? Why does Your anger smoke against the sheep of Your pasture? Remember Your congregation, which You have purchased of old, the tribe of Your inheritance, which You have redeemed—This Mount Zion where You have dwelt.*" I believe the Lord included the psalms in our Bibles to help us pray the prayers which need to be rising from the depth of our souls. The Psalms deal with so many topics and therefore can provide a prayer cover for most of the challenging issues in our natural lives as well as those in our spirits and souls. I like to pray them for what they are and to pray them as I press through my issues. I recommend the same for you.

Ask yourself a few important spiritual questions. Have you at times felt abandoned by significant people in your life? Have you sought in frustration for the intervention of the Lord, but have not yet received it? Have you cried out at night for the Lord to step in and defend your cause? Then this psalm may truly speak to your soul. Pray the prayer below aloud and let it speak out your deepest feelings and petitions to the Lord in this season and for this generation. Remember that praying the prayers we are given in the Word of God releases once again His awesome power, grace, and provision for you in this season of the harvest.

We do not see our signs; There is no longer any prophet; nor is there any among us who knows how long. O God, how long will the adversary reproach? Will the enemy blaspheme Your name forever? Why do You withdraw Your hand, even Your right hand? Take it out of Your bosom and destroy them. For God is my King from of old, working salvation in the midst of the earth. You divided the sea by Your strength; You broke the heads of the sea serpents in the waters. You broke the heads of Leviathan in pieces, and gave him as food to the people inhabiting the wilderness. You broke open the fountain and the flood; You dried up mighty rivers. The day is Yours, the night also is Yours; You have prepared the light and the sun. You have set all the borders of the earth; You have made summer and winter. Remember this, that the enemy has reproached, O Lord, and that a foolish people has blasphemed Your name. Oh, do not deliver the life of Your turtledove to the wild beast! Do not forget the life of Your poor forever. Have respect to the covenant; for the dark places of the earth are full of the haunts of cruelty. Oh, do not let the oppressed return ashamed! Let the poor and needy praise Your name. Arise, O God, plead Your own cause; remember how the foolish man reproaches You daily. (Psalm 74:9-22)

SELAH QUESTIONS

(Selah means to pause and meditate on these things.)

1. Can you think of something you have lost which you sincerely desire to have once again?

_____

_____

_____

2. What did Job fear the most?

_____

_____

_____

3. What does the experience of Job say to you about the Lord's restoration?

_____

_____

_____

4. Describe a way in which the Lord has assured you of restoring lost things.

_____

_____

_____

5. What is the meaning of the double portion and how does it speak of your relationship with the Lord.

_____

_____

_____

6. How have you let your circumstances block you from your double portion?

_____

_____

_____

CHAPTER THIRTEEN

More Restoration Promises

Isaiah 41:10, 13-15 and Zephaniah 3:9, 11-12, 17-20

T hroughout the Bible, the Father continued to make powerful "I will" promises over His people for their restoration. In the book of Isaiah, the Lord released another set of seven powerful restoration promises. In this revelation of the Lord, the promises He released are somewhat different from those we have been studying in the book of Ezekiel. One reason for the difference may be that the promises given through Isaiah were only to be activated during a future time of restoration. Therefore we can say with confidence that they were released during the time of Isaiah for our time. They were given to us in our generation. Think about it this way: we are now living in the generation which can access and activate these powerful restoration promises. Now is the time for you to receive these promises and activate them in your life and ministry.

Compare the promises released through Isaiah with the promises from Ezekiel 36. In Ezekiel, all the promises were made available to that generation as well as in the present time for our generation. Through Ezekiel, the Lord released these promises just before He gave the powerful and well-known message of a great miracle. This miracle is explained in Chapter 37 of the book of Ezekiel. In the biblical story of this miraculous restoration, we see that the Lord raised extremely dry bones back to life as a mighty army in a place we call the valley of dry bones. In this symbolic act of restoration, the Lord revealed more of Himself and His true character to all the earth. He let us know that He is the God who restores and He is powerful enough to resurrect His people in due season. Even when there is nothing left of the hopes and dreams of His people, He restores. Even when there is nothing left but some old dry bones, the Lord can bring about a great resurrection, restoration, and revival for His people.

> So they will say, 'This land that was desolate has become like the garden of Eden; and the wasted, desolate, and ruined cities are now fortified and inhabited.' Then the nations which are left all around you shall know that I, the Lord, have rebuilt the ruined places and planted what was desolate. I, the Lord, have spoken it, and I will do it." (Ezekiel 36:35-36)

There is no limit to what the Lord can do. There is no limit to what He will do for people who put their trust in Him. In the illustration of the dry bones, we see first that the Lord commanded Ezekiel to prophesy over the mountains of

Israel. This command is given in Ezekiel Chapter 36. Now think about this. Ezekiel was in captivity hundreds of miles from Israel, but his powerful God-given decrees opened and began to release a season of blessing and restoration. The land began to be made ready for the return of the Lord's people. Next, notice that in Ezekiel Chapter 37 these promises of restoration are first delivered to the people in the spiritual realm. The promises are sevenfold as are the promises of redemption given in the book of Exodus. In the same way that the Lord made those ancient promises of redemption given through Moses available to you and me, He also made these promises of restoration released in Ezekiel 36 available to us. If you haven't already done so, I recommend that you receive them and activated them by faith in your own life and ministry now.

> *Thus says the Lord God: "I will also let the house of Israel inquire of Me to do this for them: I will increase their men like a flock. Like a flock offered as holy sacrifices, like the flock at Jerusalem on its feast days, so shall the ruined cities be filled with flocks of men. Then they shall know that I am the Lord."* (Ezekiel 36:37-38)

RESTORATION PROMISES IN ISAIAH

One of the ways the Lord makes it clear that these promises of restoration are available to us is by continuing to release them in the biblical accounts of succeeding generations. This way we know that they were not just for one group in one generation, but all of us regardless of the time and circumstances in which we live. Through the prophet Isaiah, the Lord released another set of seven powerful promises of restoration. As noted above they were given as His promises for a future time of restoration. Here is the good news, the first of the promised future times came. They were released to the generation which returned to Israel from their time of captivity. But the promises didn't end there. Otherwise, there would be no reason to include them in our scriptures. They were intended for another future generation, and we are now living in that season. Once again the promises are being released to the Lord's people in this generation and they are now available to you and me.

This is how we can understand what the Lord is doing. Once His promises are released, they become available for all future generations. In this powerful word of the Lord given through Isaiah, Father God has decreed a greater level of restoration than those given to previous generations. Now, these greater promises are available to us in the present time. Once again He shows us that He gives increase more and more to us and our descendants. Read the promises given through Isaiah in the two passages below. Next, claim them for yourself and those you care for. Remember the steps for activating His promises. Speak them aloud to release God's power. Then begin to give Him praise and glory while you wait for them to manifest.

> *Fear not, for I am with you; be not dismayed, for I am your God. **I will** strengthen you, yes, **I will** help*

*you, **I will** uphold you with My righteous right hand.*
(Isaiah 41:10)

People often share with me that they don't feel strong enough or good enough to receive these three amazing promises. You need to remember two very important facts which are revealed in the passage above. It is the Lord who strengthens us. It isn't about how strong we are, but how mighty He is. It is not a matter of our righteousness, but His. His righteous right hand is with you to work all these amazing promises in your life, your family, and your ministry. Trust the Lord. He will strengthen you exactly as He has promised. He will help you and uphold you through all your challenging circumstances. Don't let doubts rob you of your promises from the Lord. The second passage filled with the "I will" promises from the Lord and released through Isaiah follows:

*For **I**, the Lord your God, **will hold** your right hand, saying to you, 'Fear not, **I will** help you.' "Fear not, you worm Jacob, you men of Israel! **I will** help you," says the Lord and your Redeemer, the Holy One of Israel. "Behold, **I will** make you into a new threshing sledge with sharp teeth; you shall thresh the mountains and beat them small, and make the hills like chaff. (Isaiah 41:13-15)*

A promise which has not been activated has little effect now or in the future. You must take the step of faith needed to release the power embedded in the promises. Only then is the power of God released to confirm the promises. Every promise of the Lord is filled with the potential to accomplish what He has spoken. His Words never return to Him without accomplishing His purposes. Read the passage below several times. Remember to read it aloud for full effect. Then consider how the Lord is making all these things available to you. There is no power on earth which can block the Lord's spoken purposes. On the other hand, you can reject them and they will not manifest in your life and work.

> "*So shall my word be that goeth forth out of my mouth: it shall not return unto me void, but it shall accomplish that which I please, and it shall prosper in the thing whereto I sent it.*" (Isaiah 55:11, KJV).

I remind you once again about the potential released when you speak the Word of God aloud. More is released as you speak it over and over. Also, this repetition anchors the promises in your heart and builds your faith to receive them. Remember once again what Paul said in Romans 10:17, "*So then faith comes by hearing, and hearing by the word of God.*" You hear it when you speak it aloud and this releases the power and potential of these promises in your life in this generation. You have the spiritual authority which has been given to you by the Lord. Listen to what Yeshua is saying in Luke 10:19, "*Behold, I give you the authority to trample on serpents and scorpions, and over all the power of the enemy, and nothing shall by any means hurt you.*" You can use the spiritual authority given by Yeshua to release the power of God in His promises and to activate His promises for you, in you and through you. Amen?

MORE RESTORATION PROMISES

In another generation, the Lord released more of His powerful restoration promises. As the Lord speaks these things over and over to various groups at various times, we are allowed to know them. The Lord wants to release them to you and me because He desires to strengthen our faith. The reason He strengthens our faith is so that we are enabled to receive even more. He is the God of restoration. This is who He is and this is what He does. He has done it over and over in the past, and we can be confident that He will do the same for you and me in our generation. Is your faith growing yet? Let it grow stronger as you read the promises given through the prophet Zephaniah. This time the Lord releases nine restoration promises to us. As we read about these promises we are reminded that He gives more and more to those He loves; those who put their trust in Him. Prophetically, the number nine speaks of divine completeness.

> For then **_I will_** restore to the peoples a pure language,
> that they all may call on the name of the Lord, to
> serve Him with one accord. (Zephaniah 3:9)

Have you ever wondered what that "pure language" will be when this promise is released? Will it be a new language never known to humans before? I know some people who think English will be spoken. What do you think? We become comfortable with our native language and tend to think it is best. My mind was changed when I began to study Hebrew. I discovered that it is a language perfectly designed to communicate the revelations of the Lord. Perhaps the new language will be Hebrew in its original form. Meanwhile, we look again at the Lord's promises given through Zephaniah.

> *In that day you shall not be shamed for any of your deeds in which you transgress against Me; For then **I will** take away from your midst those who rejoice in your pride, and you shall no longer be haughty in My holy mountain. **I will** leave in your midst a meek and humble people, and they shall trust in the name of the Lord.* (Zephaniah 3:11-12)

Do these promises sound good to you as you read them aloud over and over? I have no idea how many people want to live the way described in these promises, but I can tell you that I do. How about you? Imagine a time when no one feels shame because the Lord has brought about a great restoration. Imagine living with people who are all meek and humble. Imagine living with a group of people who all trust the Lord and desire to please Him. Imagine being a part of a group that wants to live as He has promised. It sounds too good to be true, but the fact is that it is true. When the Lord promises to do something, He will do it. We can look forward to it now as we wait for it to manifest. Amen?

> *Adonai your God is right there with you, as a mighty savior; He will rejoice over you and be glad, he will not be silent in his love, he will shout over you with joy. "**I will** gather those of yours who grieve over the appointed feasts, and bear the burden of reproach*

*[because they cannot keep them]. When that time comes, **I will** deal with all those who oppress you; **I will** save her who is lame, gather her who was driven away, and make them whose shame spread over the earth the object of praise and renown. When that time comes, **I will** bring you in, when that time comes, **I will** gather you; and make you the object of fame and praise among all the peoples of the earth – when **I restore** your fortunes before your very eyes,"* says Adonai. (Zephaniah 3:17-20, CJB)

A time is coming when the Lord will restore our fortunes before our own eyes. Are you ready for it? Are you ready to activate these promises and begin now to live the way the Lord planned for you from the beginning of time? Are you ready to accomplish His purpose in your life and reach your destiny in the Kingdom of God? Remember: the Lord has promised and He will do it. Some of these promises are obviously for another time and another season. They will manifest as the Lord wills and as He has planned, but I pray that we will not be a roadblock to this promised move of God. Now is the time to establish a plan to be obedient and responsive to the Lord as He does this amazing work for us. Amen?

COMPLETED IN YESHUA

Praying near the end of His ministry in the flesh, Yeshua said, "*I have glorified You on the earth. I have finished the work which You have given Me to do.*" (John 17:4) In other words,

Yeshua had completed all the tasks the Lord had asked Him to do. He spoke all the words the Lord told Him to release to us. He has fulfilled all that the prophets had spoken about Him in the past. Now the work of restoration is complete in the spiritual realm and can be activated by us in the natural realm. Consider John 19:30, *"So when Jesus had received the sour wine, He said, "It is finished!" And bowing His head, He gave up His spirit."* This is so important for us to understand that I want to say it again in different words hoping it will anchor in our spirits. Too often people hear the words of the Lord, but don't fully commit to them. Repetition is good and it is necessary as we teach about the Kingdom of God.

On the cross, Yeshua cried out, *"It is finished!"* All those things the Father had asked Him to do for us had been completed. He had fulfilled all the Biblical promises about His birth, life, ministry, and sacrificial death. He had fulfilled all the tough requirements of the law. He had fixed all spiritual issues which were broken in past generations. He had established a body of believers to continue His work until the end of time. Truly, it was finished along with and through all the pain He had suffered for us. So what do we need to do to deserve such a sacrifice? This is what Jesus said when He was asked these questions: *"Then they asked him, 'What must we do to do the works God requires?' Jesus answered, 'The work of God is this: to believe in the one he has sent.'"* (John 6:28-29, NIV) There it is! It is just that simple. All we have to do is believe in Him, repent and receive all He has already done for us. He has done all the hard work and carried all the heavy burdens. He did it for us because He loves us. Isn't this amazing and wonderful?

"It is finished!" All the hard work has been done for us. His victory in completing the work given to Him is then attributed to those who follow Him and have united with Him in faith. We can also become fully aware that it has been accomplished in the lives of all His followers. Each time we see it, we receive another prophetic assurance that it has all been done for us. Think about it. All of his followers abandoned Him in the garden. Peter failed three times to acknowledge that he knew the Lord. We look back and see that all of them were restored. The most dramatic was the restoration of Peter. Later, Peter would understand fully and speak for us the words in the passage below. He speaks of a time when this will all manifest in the lives of all the believers from every generation. It is all available to us today and the complete fulfillment will manifest when the Lord returns.

> *Repent therefore and be converted, that your sins may be blotted out, so that times of refreshing may come from the presence of the Lord, and that He may send Jesus Christ, who was preached to you before, whom heaven must receive until the times of restoration of all things, which God has spoken by the mouth of all His holy prophets since the world began.* (Acts 3:19-21)

When Yeshua spoke of this to the disciples, they were still unable to fully understand it or to receive it by faith. It was after the Lord breathed the Holy Spirit into them that they were enabled to fully understand these powerful Kingdom concepts. An old prophecy had declared that all things would be restored at the coming of Elijah. In their minds, this was not yet available. They didn't believe it could happen until the Lord opened their minds and told them that Elijah had already come. This prophecy was about John the Baptizer. I also believe it was fulfilled when Peter, James, and John saw Elijah on the Mount of Transfiguration. I believe this was given for them and for us to understand that the work is truly finished and all we need to do is receive it and activate it. Amen?

> *Jesus answered and said to them, "Indeed, Elijah is coming first and **will restore all things**. But I say to you that Elijah has come already, and they did not know him but did to him whatever they wished. Likewise the Son of Man is also about to suffer at their hands." Then the disciples understood that He spoke to them of John the Baptist.* (Matthew 17:11-13)

ACTIVATION

I pointed out earlier that the Lord had given some powerful and visual means for the people to remember His "I will" promises. He continues to do this to help us understand and activate the promises of redemption through teachings included in the Passover Haggadah (see my book, "Redemption, Seven "I Will" promises of the Lord"). The four cups used in the Seder meal along with the words associated with them were clear reminders of the redemption won for us by the Lord. These promises and their fulfillment were to be considered at least once every year during the season of Passover. Some Hebrew scholars believe the four corners of the Prayer Shawl are a daily reminder of the four main promises of redemption. In the same way, the Lord gave the Hebrew people the "*mikvah*" (cleansing through immersion in water) ritual. These are all means the Lord uses to constantly remind us of His powerful promises. We can also use them the same way in our generation so that we will never forget the great things the Lord has done for us. We are also helped in understanding that the Lord still keeps all His promises. Not even one of His promises will fail. In the future, as you celebrate the Lord's Passover, let these words be a reminder of the faithfulness and power of the Lord. Amen?

In our generation, we are invited to remember the Lord's restoration promises in Christian baptism. In our baptism, we see and experience a powerful revelation of the Lord's work. In the natural, He cleanses us on the outside and then on the inside. We see the outward sign of the water and experience the inner spiritual work of the Lord. But it doesn't end here. Later as we witness the baptisms of others who are being added to the body of believers these teachings are brought to memory and are being reinforced in us once again. Each time a believer is baptized we are reminded that it is the Lord who cleanses us. Think about it. In this way, He is enabling us to access His gifts and grace over and over. He is preparing us for an amazing and powerful restoration.

The Lord continues to do this work for us in many different ways to help us understand, receive, and activate His promises of restoration. Each time we see this manifest, we are reminded of His promises and we have the opportunity to increase our faith. Tragically, many people get jealous of the restoration in another person's life and separate themselves from the source which can release it to them. Jealousy is probably the greatest inhibiter to the release of the Lord's promises. When you see someone receive a mighty move of restoration, celebrate with them, and then say for yourself: "I am next!" A positive response increases your openness to receive what the Lord has for you, but a jealous response will block your ability to see and receive. Do not let a spirit of jealousy rule over you. Together we come into agreement to break off this spirit and all its effects on us in the mighty name of Yeshua ha Messiach.

The prophet Micah lived during challenging times when people had lost so much both physically and spiritually because of their unfaithfulness to the Lord. Can you imagine how they felt toward their captors who treated them so badly? While enemies gloated over him, Micah made some decrees which I believe helped him to activate the Lord's promises in His own life. There is a wide range of emotions released in the passage below, but I want you to focus on his faith statements. He knew that the bad times would end. He had complete faith in the Lord that a time of restoration was close at hand. He was trying to get ready for it. He wanted to build a faith that could receive and activate the Lord's promises of restoration. In other words, he knew that the Lord's mercy and justice were close at hand and would soon manifest. Read his words aloud and let your faith grow to understand that no matter how dire your circumstances may be, you are on the edge of a mighty move of God which will fully restore you. Amen?

> But as for me, **I will** **look to Adonai**; **I will** **wait for the God** of my salvation; my God will hear me. Enemies of mine, don't gloat over me! Although I have fallen, **I will rise**; though I live in the dark, Adonai is my light. **I will endure Adonai's rage**, because I sinned against Him, until He pleads my cause and judges in my favor. Then he will bring me out to the light; and **I will see His justice**. My enemies will see it too, and shame will cover those who said to me, "Where is Adonai your God?" **I will gloat over them**, as they are trampled underfoot like mud in the streets. (Micah 7:7-10, CJB)

SELAH QUESTIONS

(Selah means to pause and meditate on these things.)

1. How can you prepare to receive the promises of restoration in your life?

_____

_____

_____

2. What does it mean when the Lord says things over and over?

_____

_____

_____

3. What new element of restoration did you understand better through Isaiah?

_____

_____

_____

4. How does speaking the promises aloud increase their potential?

_____

_____

_____

5. How did the message given through the prophet Zephaniah help you to build your faith?

_____

_____

_____

6. On the cross, what did Yeshua mean when He said, "It is finished!"?

_____

_____

_____

7. What did you learn from Micah's declarations?

_____

_____

_____

CHAPTER FOURTEEN

Restoration Gathering

I n many Television shows and old movies, we have been introduced to people who are relentlessly searching through ancient manuscripts, old maps, local legends, and nearly forgotten folklore in search of hidden treasure or to understand great mysteries or to uncover ancient wisdom. They travel from location to location in hopes of solving some great mystery that has plagued treasure hunters for years. We cheer with them as they diligently search in hopes of finding some long-forgotten location where people of a former generation have hidden vast treasures of gold or jewels. If you have watched any of the documentary forms of these shows, you know that these people seldom find anything. Yet somehow they are driven to continue the pursuit regardless of the cost.

Despite their constant failures, many of these people continue to search. It is as if they have been intoxicated by the excitement of the challenges involved in the search and they just continue drinking at the well of hopelessness. In other words, some of these people appear to be somehow addicted to the search. They spend countless hours searching, digging, and chasing the elusive promise of hidden treasure. In the meantime, they lose family, friends, and fortunes. Yet they remain committed to this vain search for human glory. It is sad to see them experience failure after failure while giving up the fortune and family they already have. Knowing all this, I still want you to begin a search of your own.

> *Again, the kingdom of heaven is like treasure hidden in a field, which a man found and hid; and for joy over it he goes and sells all that he has and buys that field. Again, the kingdom of heaven is like a merchant seeking beautiful pearls, who, when he had found one pearl of great price, went and sold all that he had and bought it.* (Matthew 13:44-46)

I want you to risk everything as you seek the "pearl of great price" and the hidden treasure in the open fields of God's promises. As you search, remember that unlike the seekers we spoke of earlier, you are assured that with the Lord you will never fail to receive all the good things He has promised to you. I want this for you because there is one very special treasure which is real and we can all find it if we seek it with our whole heart. Remember the promised blessing in Psalm 119:2, *"Blessed are those who keep His testimonies, who seek Him with the whole heart!* I want you to know about an ancient manuscript with very specific guidance on how to find the greatest treasure in the Universe – Eternal life in Yeshua ha Messiach. Look closely at Psalm 24:5-6, *"He shall receive blessing from the Lord, and righteousness from the God of his salvation. This is Jacob, the generation of those who seek Him, who seek Your face."* I want you to find your very special treasure which has been promised to you. I want you to receive the great restoration He has promised to all who seek His face. Believe the promise of Yeshua released in the passage below. Receive it and activate it now. The Lord has prepared it for you, your family, and your ministry.

> *So Jesus said to them, "Assuredly I say to you, that in the regeneration, when the Son of Man sits on the throne of His glory, you who have followed Me will also sit on twelve thrones, judging the twelve tribes of Israel. And everyone who has left houses or brothers or sisters or father or mother or wife or children or lands, for My name's sake, shall receive a hundred-fold, and inherit eternal life.* (Matthew 19:28-29)

Did you notice that this promise is for both now in this present age as well as in the age to come? Some people think about eternal life as something far away and unattainable in the present age. This is not what the Word of God teaches. As soon as we come into a saving relationship with Yeshua, we enter into eternal life. We are no longer bound by the natural body living in fear of death. We have already died with Christ and we have also been raised with Him. Yeshua taught this and many of the people who lived in His day believed it was something new. Consider the passage below and see that this has been the Lord's plan all along.

For thus says the Lord: 'Just as I have brought all this great calamity on this people, so I will bring on them all the good that I have promised them. And fields will be bought in this land of which you say, "It is desolate, without man or beast; it has been given into the hand of the Chaldeans." Men will buy fields for money, sign deeds and seal them, and take witnesses, in the land of Benjamin, in the places around Jerusalem, in the cities of Judah, in the cities of the mountains, in the cities of the lowland, and in the cities of the South; for I will cause their captives to return,' says the Lord." (Jeremiah 32:42-44)

Many people today are like those who listened to Yeshua teach. Most of them have never been taught and have no idea that the Lord has planned from the beginning of time to give them their promised restoration. These ideas are not new although they are new to these people. Other people have been taught about these promises, but have believed they were only given once ages ago and are no longer available to people in our generation. Both of these groups of people are inaccurate in their beliefs. All of these things promised long ago are still available to the Lord's people today. Never let your doubts prevent you from receiving and activating the Lord's restoration promises for your life and the lives of those you care for.

I WILL RETURN AND REBUILD

The Lord keeps making these powerful "I will" promises of restoration throughout the scriptures. The problem is that people continue to doubt and then fail to fully receive and activate them. Don't make that mistake. Believe His Word! Believe His promises. Trust that He will do what He says He will do. This is not just an old story with no meaning for people today. These are the eternal promises of God that are available to all generations of His children. They are as much for you as they were for the children of Israel when first spoken. The Lord directed that these promises be included in His Word because they could be released to people in the future. They were given for people today who read them, believe them, receive them, and activate them. Now it is your task to receive them in your generation. Notice that the promises in the passage below were given for people in the future. Their future is our present time. Don't let doubt block you from receiving what the Lord has promised to you. Trust the Lord and be blessed!

> *I will gather those who sorrow over the appointed assembly, who are among you, to whom its reproach is a burden. Behold, at that time I will deal with all who afflict you; I will save the lame, and gather those who were driven out; I will appoint them for praise and fame in every land where they were put to shame. At that time I will bring you back, even at the time I gather you; for I will give you fame and praise among all the peoples of the earth, when I*

return your captives before your eyes, says the Lord.
(Zephaniah 3:18-20)

Some people still read passages of scripture like the one above and think these promises were only spoken over the Children of Israel and were only available in the distant past. Because of this belief, they fail to reach out to receive and activate them in their own lives. Don't make that mistake. The church has not replaced Israel as the object of the Father's love but has been included by the awesome work of Yeshua ha Messiach. It is no longer a case of either/or. It has become a case of both/ and. One of the main contributions of the ministry of the Apostle Paul was to provide a greater understanding of these things for you and me. Look carefully at the passage below and increase your faith to receive and activate all of the Lord's promises in your life.

> *The whole assembly became silent as they listened to Barnabas and Paul telling about the miraculous signs and wonders God had done among the Gentiles through them. When they finished, James spoke up: "Brothers, listen to me. Simon has described to us how God at first showed his concern by taking from the Gentiles a people for himself. The words of the prophets are in agreement with this, as it is written: "After this **I will return** and rebuild David's fallen tent. Its ruins **I will rebuild**, and **I will restore it**, that the remnant of men may seek the Lord, and **all the Gentiles who bear my name**, says the Lord,*

who does these things' that have been known for ages.
(Acts 15:12-18, NIV)

When the Lord decreed that He would return and restore David's fallen tent, Paul clearly understood and established for us that these promises included the "Gentiles" among their numbers then and all of us now. If you bear the name of Yeshua, you are promised all these glorious things. If you are not certain about where you stand on these issues, this is a great opportunity to accept Yeshua as your Lord and Savior. All you need to do is make a confession of your sins and ask Him to keep His promises in your life. Ask Him to become Lord in your life and release all His promises to you. He has already done all the spiritual work necessary for you to be included. All you have to do is accept His gracious invitation.

UNITY IS OUR KEY

If you want to unlock the door to all these promises, the Lord has released a powerful key that will open all these things for you. The location of this key has not been hidden now or in past generations. Unity is the highest goal of our faith. In John 14:23, Yeshua said it this way: *"Jesus answered and said unto him, if a man love me, he will keep my words: and my Father will love him, and we will come unto him, and make our abode with him."* This unity begins when we love and obey the Lord. When we come into this powerful unity with the Father and the Son, the promise is that they will abide with us. Then the unity is extended toward other believers. In John

15:12, Yeshua said it this way: "*This is My commandment, that you love one another as I have loved you.*" Unity is the key to unlock these promises of the Lord. Paul taught the church in Ephesus that this is the plan the Lord has made for us.

> *And He Himself gave some to be apostles, some prophets, some evangelists, and some pastors and teachers, for the equipping of the saints for the work of ministry, for the edifying of the body of Christ,* **till we all come to the unity** *of the faith and of the knowledge of the Son of God, to a perfect man, to the measure of the stature of the fullness of Christ;* (Ephesians 4:11-13)

The Psalmist knew and understood that unity opens the way for the Lord to manifest more powerfully in our lives. In the teaching described in the passage below, we know that unity results in the Lord commanding a blessing for us. Unity is the key to receiving the promise of "*life for evermore.*" Rid yourself of everything which blocks unity in your life and work. If you need to forgive and restore others, don't hesitate to do it. Unforgiveness does not provide any benefit to you. It harms you in spirit, soul, and body. Let go of these negative feelings so you can receive the fullness of the blessing of the Lord. Amen?

> *Behold, how good and how pleasant it is for brethren to dwell together in unity! It is like the precious ointment upon the head, that ran down upon the beard, even Aaron's beard: that went down to the skirts of*

his garments; As the dew of Hermon, and as the dew that descended upon the mountains of Zion: for there the Lord commanded the blessing, even life for evermore. (Psalm 133:1-3, KJV)

David understood how powerful unity is and gave this very descriptive lesson about it. This appears to be a reference to Aaron's anointing as the High Priest of the people. Having Aaron in this position was a great source of unity among the people. Has your anointing brought unity and peace to those around you? Perhaps David's imagery is a little too old to make it clear for you. Here is a challenge. Think about your image of this kind of unity and write this passage for your understanding. What would make you feel certain that unity is good and pleasant in your life and work? Then activate the promise of receiving *"life for evermore."*

BEING ENABLED

Look into your inmost being and ask yourself: Are you spiritually disabled? This appears to be the main message in the passage below. The Lord gives a new "I will" promise. He will enable those who are not fully able to fit into the new circumstances He is about to release. At times it is very challenging to live in unity with others. To do this and to live in the ways the Lord has called us to live, love, and work together, (we and others) probably need some divine enabling.

It is also clear in this teaching that you cannot enable yourself. You need a mighty work of the Lord to be enabled to receive His greatest blessings. As you study this passage, think about all that the Lord can and will restore for you. The Lord speaks it and then proclaims that He will do it for you. Amen? Perhaps the reason you have not fully grasped all these things in the past is because of your disability. Don't despair. The Lord says He is ready and willing to enable you. Receive it now.

> *Thus says the Lord God: "On the day that I cleanse you from all your iniquities, **I will** also **enable** you to dwell in the cities, and the ruins shall be rebuilt. The desolate land shall be tilled instead of lying desolate in the sight of all who pass by. So they will say, 'This land that was desolate has become like the Garden of Eden; and the wasted, desolate, and ruined cities are now fortified and inhabited.' Then the nations which are left all around you shall know that I, the Lord, have rebuilt the ruined places and planted what was desolate. **I, the Lord, have spoken it, and I will do it.**"* (Ezekiel 36:33-36)

The Lord says something truly amazing in the passage below. He will permit you to ask these things of Him. In some periods of history, the rebellion of His people was so great that He put these promises on hold and only agreed to release them in some future generation. This is not the case now. You may ask: How is this possible? It is possible because it is the Lord's work and He has permitted you to ask to understand your role and to understand how and what He plans to do in your generation, in your life, and your ministry. When He spoke this to His people through Ezekiel, they didn't have Yeshua as a guide and example. Thanks be to the Father that we have Yeshua ha Messiach.

A new spiritual season has risen for us because of the work of Yeshua ha Messiach. Now is the time to seek to understand it and to be enabled to do it. Think about it. This is the appointed time to ask the Lord to release all these restoration promises in your life. Are you ready to receive them? If you are ready, read the passage below aloud and let the promises of the Lord flow to you and through you to bless others. Amen? By the manifestation of these things, we will all know that He is Adonai. This is one of our great evangelistic tools provided by the Lord. The increase given by the Lord will put the world in shock and awe. When this manifests, people will see what they thought was impossible. Amen?

> *Thus says the Lord God: "**I will** also let the house of Israel inquire of Me to do this for them: **I will** increase their men like a flock. Like a flock offered as holy sacrifices, like the flock at Jerusalem on its feast days, so shall the ruined cities be filled with flocks of men. Then they shall know that I am the Lord."*
> (Ezekiel 36:37-38)

ACTIVATION

As you receive these powerful promises of God, let the scriptures show you additional ways to receive and activate them. Praise is the main key to activating the promises. Praise releases the power inherent in each of the promises. Begin now to praise Him and prepare now for a fresh new activation in your life and work. Pray these prayers aloud over yourself, your family, and your ministry. Amen? The passage below is provided to assist you in giving wholehearted praise to the Lord.

> *Make a joyful shout to the Lord, all you lands! Serve the Lord with gladness; Come before His presence with singing. Know that the Lord, He is God; it is He who has made us, and not we ourselves; we are His people and the sheep of His pasture. Enter into His gates with thanksgiving, and into His courts with praise. Be thankful to Him, and bless His name. For the Lord is good; His mercy is everlasting, and His truth endures to all generations. (Psalm 100:1-5)*

Praise is a powerful key for opening the way for the Lord's promises and blessings to flow into your life and work for His Kingdom. Praise is like the password which opens the gates and allows you to enter. One very important fact to remember is that praise is not dependent on your feelings or your current circumstances. You must break free from the tyranny of letting your circumstances determine your blessings. When you feel the least desire to give praise, it is the most important time to do it.

Let your praises be based on faith and not on fear or frustration. Release your God-given faith to overcome whatever hinders your praise. This is how you become a victor in all circumstances. This is how you become a praise warrior for the Lord. Picture in your mind the praise team leading the troops into battle as in the days of Jehoshaphat. Before they reached the front lines, the Lord had already won a victory for them. Now it is your turn to operate in faith in the same way the great heroes of the past were enabled to share in the Lord's victories. Now is the time to receive, activate, and release the power of the Lord's promises. Amen?

SELAH QUESTIONS

(Selah means to pause and meditate on these things.)

1. What is your heart longing for right now?

_____

_____

_____

2. Is your heart longing for a closer walk with the Lord?

_____

_____

_____

3. Describe how you are seeking His face today.

_____

_____

_____

4. Can you name something you have sought above all else in your life?

_____

_____

_____

5. Describe how these promises are both for now and in eternity.

_____

_____

_____

6. How has the Lord included you in all His promises?

_____

_____

_____

7. What is the role of unity in activating the promises of the Lord?

_____

_____

_____

8. In what ways have you been enabled to receive these promises of the Lord?

_____

_____

_____

Summary

The Lord promises over and over to each successive generation that He will restore both natural and spiritual things that His people have lost. We have many great testimonies in the Bible proving that the Lord kept these promises for His people in these past generations. Yet many of His people today have little if any faith in His powerful promises. Some just ignore them because they have not been taught to know or understand their significance. Others believe that these promises of restoration are reserved for the end of time. These people don't understand that they can activate them now and live today in the manifestation of these great promises of the Lord. Think about what David meant when he said, "*I am still confident of this: I will see the goodness of the Lord in the land of the living.*" (Psalm 27:13, NIV) He believed that the promises of the Lord would manifest for him during his lifetime on the earth. Now it is our turn to have this kind of faith and to be fully confident that the Lord will keep His promises to us during our lifetimes.

Where do you stand concerning the promises of the Lord for restoration? Do you believe them with all your heart? Are you faithfully waiting in expectancy for all of them to manifest in your life? Have you taken steps to activate them as described in this book as well as in the scriptures? Don't lose heart. Don't give up moments before the manifestation of the Lord's promises in your life. Stand firm in your faith. Remember what Paul said about standing in Ephesians 6:13, "*Therefore take up the whole armor of God, that you may be able to withstand in the evil day, and having done all, to stand.*" When you have done all you can do to stand, what do you do? You keep on standing with the Lord. As in the days of Jehoshaphat, Just suit up and show up as you watch the Lord win a great victory for you. Amen?

So many people I talk to believe that they will only receive these promises when they get to heaven. Here is a thought. You won't need most of them in Heaven, because the Lord will be in charge of all things and you will live in perfect Shalom. You need the things the Lord promised in this present time and for the spiritual battles you are engaged in now. It is the Lord's plan for you to see them manifest now, and to let them enable you to do all that He has included in your purpose and destiny for the Kingdom of God. Think about that as you read the passage below. Like the psalmist, take heart with the full assurance that you will see the goodness of the Lord in the land of the living. Amen? Look closely at this more complete message from Davin in Psalm Twenty Seven.

I would have lost heart, unless I had believed that I would see the goodness of the Lord in the land of the living. Wait on the Lord; be of good courage, and He shall strengthen your heart; wait, I say, on the Lord! (Psalm 27:13-14)

As I continued through this study, something began to stand out for me in a new and more powerful way. Promises of restoration are given repeatedly. These promises are spoken more often than almost any others in the Word of God. There is something very special about the Lord's desire to restore things in your life and ministry. He is really serious about this. How about you? Are you equally determined to receive and activate them? Many of us need to shed the blankets of doubt covering our eyes and our spirits. Then we need to rise again filled with faith in the Lord's ability and willingness to keep these promises for us. These coverings of doubt which block our faith were likely given to us by people in previous generations. My advice to you is to let go of every doubt-filled idea you have been taught, and believe what the Lord says! Believe what He promises! Believe that He wants to give you these things in your generation. Put your trust in Him. Amen?

One of the most familiar passages about the Lord's plan for restoration is in the Biblical quote below. Most of us are familiar with it. We have heard it spoken over and over in the past. The question is: Do we believe this is for us? Would the Lord do all this for you and me? As you study this passage, read it over and over again. Speak it aloud until it takes root in your heart. Read it until you have more faith in this promise than any words of doubt imparted to you in the past. Make it yours right now. Believe it. Receive it. Activate it in your life and ministry right now. Amen?

> So **I will restore** to you the years that the swarming locust has eaten, the crawling locust, the consuming locust, and the chewing locust, My great army which I sent among you. You shall eat in plenty and be satisfied, and praise the name of the Lord your God, Who has dealt wondrously with you; and My people shall never be put to shame. Then you shall know that I am in the midst of Israel: I am the Lord your God and there is no other. My people shall never be put to shame. (Joel 2:25-27)

I love this collection of promises released through the prophet Joel. All these promised spiritual gifts began to manifest on the day of Shavuot (Pentecost) when the power of the Holy Spirit fell on those gathered in the Upper Room. As I have shared with you in our study, the restoration of Shavuot began in the spiritual realm first and then extended to the natural. We need to be restored spiritually and mentally if we are going to be able to receive and activate all the Lord's promises. This is why we began with what the Lord had planned and promised for our physical and spiritual cleansing. This is why the Lord needs to give us a new spirit before we can handle all the rest of His amazing restoration promises. Peter understood this because the Spirit of truth had been released to him so that he was enabled to teach these powerful spiritual truths.

On that first Shavuot, Peter made it clear. Think about it as you read his words in the passage below:

> *Then Peter said to them, "Repent, and let every one of you be baptized in the name of Jesus Christ for the remission of sins; and you shall receive the gift of the Holy Spirit. For the promise is to you and to your children, and to all who are afar off, as many as the Lord our God will call."* (Acts 2:38-39)

Did you get it? The promise is for all people. You may have been "afar off" before you accepted Yeshua as your Savior. You may have thought it was too good to be true for people like you and me. Listen to Peter again, "*the promise is to you and to your children.*" Now is the time to take Peter's advice and repent. Now is the time to be baptized in the Holy Spirit. Now is the time to allow the Lord to give you two great and awesome gifts: the remission of sins and the Holy Spirit. Amen? Remember Yeshua's promise in the passage below. Read it aloud until it is anchored in your heart. Then activate it in your spirit. Let the Lord breathe a fresh anointing of His Holy Spirit on you right now. Amen?

> *I still have many things to say to you, but you cannot bear them now. However, when He, the Spirit of truth, has come, He will guide you into all truth; for He will not speak on His own authority, but whatever He hears He will speak; and He will tell you things to come. He will glorify Me, for He will take of what is Mine and declare it to you.* (John 16:12-14)

Other Books By This Author

"A Warrior's Guide to the Seven Spirits of God"–Part 1: Basic Training, by James A. Durham

"A Warrior's Guide to the Seven Spirits of God"–Part 2: Advanced Individual Training, by James A. Durham,

"Beyond the Ancient Door" – Free to Move About the Heavens, by James A. Durham

"Restoring Foundations for Intercessor Warriors" by James A. Durham

"Gatekeepers Arise!" by James A. Durham, Copyright © James A. Durham

"Seven Levels of Glory" by James A. Durham, Copyright © James A. Durham

"100 Days in Heaven" by James A. Durham, Copyright © James A. Durham

"Keys to Open Heaven" by James A. Durham, Copyright © James A. Durham

"Appointed Times" – The Signs and Seasons of Yeshua, by James A. Durham

"A Fire Falls" – Moving into Holy Spirit Fire, by James A. Durham

"Seeing the Unseen Realm" – Destinies Revealed, by James A. Durham

"7 Hidden Keys" – Unlocking Your Supernatural Mind, by James A. Durham

"Alert! Perilous Times" – A Prepper's Guide to the Last Days, by James A. Durham

"Redemption" – 7 "I Will" Promises of God, by James A. Durham

These Books plus teaching CDs and DVDs
are available online at:
www.highercallingministriesintl.com